THE GOVCON WINNERS™ WAY

How To Win Government Contracts Faster Than Trying to Do It Alone!

DR. KIZZY M. PARKS &
DR. MYRON GOLDEN

The GovCon Winners™ Way

How To Win Government Contracts Faster Than Trying to Do It Alone!

Book Design by Transcendent Publishing

ISBN: 979-8-9890682-7-2

Printed in the United States of America.

DEDICATION

To all the small business owners, aspiring business owners, and those who are curious:

Whose dreams are vast and ambitions boundless...

Whose every sunrise signifies hope and every sunset marks resilience...

This book, "THE GOVCON WINNERS™ WAY," is a testament to your indomitable spirit, your boundless courage, and your unwavering tenacity.

May your journey within the realm of federal contracting not only flourish but also inspire countless others.

For in your success, we see the true strength of our nation's entrepreneurial spirit.

#EverythingisPossible!

–Dr. Kizzy M. Parks

CONTENTS

PREFACE

Federal government contracting, a realm once perceived as the exclusive domain of giant conglomerates, has steadily opened its doors to a broader array of businesses, each bringing a unique blend of agility, innovation, and passion. However, with opportunities come challenges, and navigating this labyrinth requires more than just technical know-how. It requires understanding the unwritten rules of the game, doing the subtle dance of networking, and performing the art of positioning one's business favorably within the vast government apparatus. To help you do these things, I have shared how I have won over $50M in federal government contracts.

"THE GOVCON WINNERS™ WAY BOOK" is not just another boring book written by someone who's never really won federal government contracts. Instead, it is the culmination of experiences, lessons learned, and insights gleaned from yours truly, Dr. Kizzy M. Parks. This book aims to demystify the world of federal contracting, offering both novices and seasoned players a clear path to success. Herein, we don't just discuss the 'how-to,' but delve into the 'why,' providing readers with a holistic understanding that will empower them to anticipate challenges, seize opportunities, and, most importantly, emerge as winners in the competitive arena of government contracts.

As you read these pages, you'll uncover strategies, tools, and anecdotes that have been instrumental in shaping the careers of many successful contractors. I invite you on this journey to decode, understand, and master the GovCon arena, and to pave your own Winners' Way.

INTRODUCTION

This book WILL change your life—and that's not an exaggeration!

Each year, the federal government spends over $500 billion on small business owners like YOU! Chances are that you thought it only purchased from companies it knows, only purchased weapons, or that your company is too small to sell to it. Well, I'm here to tell you, "heck, naw!" The federal government purchases classroom training, yoga classes, administrative services, cyber security support, powdered milk, drum sets, security services, and much, much more. It does so with businesses of all kinds, worldwide, so it can get the goods and services it needs. $500 billion! That's almost too much money for our brains to comprehend. And some of that money needs to be landing in YOUR bank account!

Yes, you read that right! You, too, can bring in a portion of that money, no matter who you are, what your background, or what expertise you bring to the table. Having the federal government as a client will change your life in ways you can't imagine. For example, I'm writing this book from the balcony of my hotel suite on Waikiki Beach in Honolulu!

Why? Because I can, because I LOVE Hawaii, and because we have a six figure, five-year contract with Schofield Barracks, HI!

Here is a picture of my Hawaii team at a recent dinner event!

Imagine having a contract in Hawaii, not having to ask anyone for time off, and being able to spend more time with family and friends. All of this and more has happened in my life because of government contracting, and can happen to you, too! When it comes to contracting, there is NO (cash money) limit! Instead, #EverythingisPossible!

How far you go depends on how well you navigate the complex environment of government contracting. Like most things having to do with the federal government, it isn't easy, and there's no shortage of gurus spreading BS to make a quick dollar!

But, no worries, because NOW you have the ultimate compass: The GovCon Winners Strategy.

As of the writing of this book, I've won **well over $70 million in federal government contracts** (cue DJ Khaled, "All I do is win!"). My companies have fulfilled contracts for providing everything from Oculus headsets, video editing, staff training, staffing, recruiting, and IT services support. Today, we have well over 100 team members located worldwide, including in Egypt and England.

You simply can't win that amount in federal government contracts due to luck or having amazing curly hair, but you can thanks to The GovCon Winners® Strategy.

On the other hand, I've also *lost* millions in contracts, too. For instance, because I didn't include a signed contract document, I missed out on a billion-dollar contract! Yes, a billion, like those that Jay, Bey, and Elon are worth!

If you've made mistakes, I've made them too, and more. If you've felt discouraged, well, I wanted to quit many times and get a 9-5 job or teach full time. However, there is nothing normal about me, thank goodness: my first name is Kizzy and last name Parks! AND, there is nothing normal about YOU, either! To live an extraordinary life, you must take "Ls" sometimes, all while NEVER giving up! It is easy to be normal, but well worth it to be extraordinary, which is more than possible through federal government contracting. #EverythingisPossible!

It took me over a decade to create the legacy I've built. I started as a subcontractor specializing in Diversity and Inclusion consulting for the Defense Equal Opportunity Management Institute (DEOMI) at what is now Patrick Space Force Base, FL (see baby Kizzy with her hair pulled back in green, at left).

I didn't have a business plan, line of credit, or business credit card, and I sure didn't know how to find contracts or how to bid on them. Over the course of 10 years, I made several mistakes, got scammed, and learned a lot about what not to do! I also learned what to do from paid and unpaid mentors. I'm writing this book so that you don't have to suffer! Lockheed Martin, IBM, and Deloitte shouldn't be the only companies winning federal government contracts. YOU should be winning contracts, too!

There's no such thing as paying your dues in government contracting. I'm here sharing my wisdom with you—just as my mentors did with me—so you can build a successful business and get your money back from Uncle Sam, as the vast majority of federal contracts are funded by YOUR tax dollars!

This book will teach you everything you need to know to get started in federal contracting—as well as point out the BS you *don't* need to listen to.

Together, we'll cover:

- The basics of federal government contracting, including contract types and set-asides
- The fundamentals of growing a business through government contracts by developing your business model and understanding commodities
- How to generate leads and convert them into contract wins
- The importance of relationship building
- Online and offline marketing strategies
- How to apply what you've learned and start winning contracts

If you take away just one thing from this book, let it be that YOU are more than capable of winning contracts and earning millions. You just need to have the right mindset, a willingness to work (and work hard!), and someone who will show you the ropes. Oh...and did I mention that this someone also has cute curly hair?

If you're ready to transform your life, then strap in and let's get to work 🚀!

CHAPTER 1

THE BASICS OF GOVERNMENT CONTRACTING

Before you update your Instagram or LinkedIn profile with the title of "Government Contractor," I want to make sure we're on the same page. You may already be registered on SAM.gov (more on that later), new to government contracting, or have even won your first contract, but you wouldn't be reading this book if you knew what the heck you were doing.

I didn't know what I was doing either when I first got into government contracting.

When I was a graduate research fellow at then-Patrick Air Force Base, FL, I saw my job as a means to an end. I just wanted to make money while in graduate school and use the job as work experience. My goals at the time were to finish graduate school, land a big-girl job, pay my student loans, find that perfect man, and get married (cue Jagged Edge 🎶 🎼 🎶)!

Then, one day, I was walking down the hall minding my own business, when out of nowhere the director of research popped out and said, "*Hey, Kizzy, I heard you're graduating soon. I'd love for you to stay on as a government contractor. How much is it gonna cost me?*"

At that moment, I had no idea what he was talking about or what to say. Never in my life had I thought that my first big-girl job negotiation was going to take place in a hallway—with people listening from their cubicles on my left and right—and have something to do with this thing called government contracting. So, I just threw out a number, a number a little under $100,000. Immediately, his eyes brightened, and he yelled, "YES, I'll have my admin follow up with you."

After that conversation, I was left with so many questions. What is government contracting? What does it mean to be a contractor? What types of contracts are there? I didn't even understand how contractors get paid. Here I am below still trying to figure all of that out (center)!

I took on the challenge, however, because I knew in that moment that I wasn't meant to be small. I knew my dad, Arthur

Parks, Jr., never raised me, his baby girl, that way (see us, below)! It was my opportunity to *be* and *dream* BIG. So, I immediately got a business address, formed a S-corporation, and got a logo. Over the course of 10 long years, I sought out mentorship, went to the SBA and PTAC (more on those later), paid for classes, got scammed, and lost hundreds of millions in government contract opportunities along the way. But, I never gave up or lost faith. Instead, I continued fighting and went on to win ***over $70 million*** in government contracts!

Now, I'll share what I've learned with you so that you don't have to go through what I did to build a successful company. Instead, you've been fast tracked, like the ticket option at Disney, because the world of government contracting will change your life far beyond anything you could ever imagine. I work when and where I want to do so, I've a ton of time for my family and friends, and I've engaged in philanthropy and investing in real estate.

So, let's start by reviewing the fundamentals of government contracting, so I can help you fill in the gaps and ensure you have a solid understanding of the foundational pieces before we talk strategy. That way, you won't ever find yourself caught off guard in a hallway wondering, "what the heck is government contracting?"

Besides, if you want to become an expert at something, the first thing you have to do is master the basics, right? So, let's dive in!

What Is Government Contracting?

Defining government contracting starts with understanding how the federal government works. You may have never thought about it this way before, but it is actually the largest customer in the world!

Because the US is such a great country, with plenty of resources as well as challenges, as well as having one of the largest populations on earth, the federal government requires an enormous amount of resources to run it. And, because the government isn't itself a supplier of goods and services, it has to rely on others to provide it with the things it needs.

Therefore, government contracting involves legal agreements between a federal agency and you, the business owner, to provide it with these things. It purchases a wide variety of products and services. By law, it MUST set aside 23% of its budget for contracting to contract with small businesses. The vast majority of federal government contracts are paid for by taxpayer dollars, and as a result, it follows a variety of rules and regulations to make these contracts.

Just like you and me, the federal government buys all types of goods and services every year. But *unlike* you and me, it's spending hundreds of billions of dollars a year, and its budget is only increasing. As you can imagine, that amount of money can't all be spent in one place in the same way you can buy most everything you need at Target or Walmart. Therefore, the government looks to businesses all around the world to supply it with every type of product or service you can imagine.

The way the federal government buys from businesses is through contracts. Federal departments and agencies employ companies by proposing contracts for bid which detail the specific goods or services needed. Different companies bid on those proposed contracts, and whichever ones win, get those contracts. Once a company wins a contract, it then becomes responsible for following through on providing whatever goods or services they agreed to provide the agency.

GovCon Winners™ Mythbusting

Does being a government contractor make you a government entity?

No. It's important to know the difference between being a government contractor and a government entity.

Just because you're awarded a contract by the government doesn't mean you are part of the government or get tax or other government benefits. Unless you're a non-profit, your goal in government contracting is to make a profit—you're selling goods and services, after all. You're a *business*, and the government sees and treats you as such.

What Are the Different Types of Contracts?

There are four main types of government contracts, and each one serves the federal government's needs differently. It's important that you know what they are because each one requires a unique approach to bidding, as well as a different approach to carrying out the work in the contract.

Fixed-price contract: This type of contract provides a set, firm price for the goods or services requested. These contracts are used when the contract risk is low, and the agency and contractor can easily agree on a price ceiling, or a maximum amount the contractor is allowed to charge, for the product or service.

Cost-reimbursement contract: This type of contract ensures the contractor is reimbursed for some or all of its expenses up to a certain limit. In many cases, the contractor is also paid an additional agreed-upon amount (called a "cost-plus" contract), so that the contractor may make a profit on the contract, rather than just break even.

Time and materials contract: This type of contract allows contractors to charge for the direct labor hours and actual material costs of its work. Because time and materials contracts are a greater financial risk to the government, they're only used when it's not possible to accurately estimate the extent or duration of the work the contractor may need to provide.

Indefinite delivery/indefinite quantity (IDIQ) contract: This type of contract allows the government to be flexible about the quantity of items and labor hours listed, rather than be exact (which most contracts require). Because it's not always possible for the government to know how many items or hours of the contractor's time will be required, they often prefer to use this type of contract in that situation.

What Are the Types of Contractors?

There are two types of contractors that support the federal government: *prime contractors* and *subcontractors.*

Prime contractor (aka Prime): A prime contractor (which may be a person or a company) has the contract with the government, is typically the main point of contact with the government, and has an active CAGE Code in SAM.gov. If you bid on and win a contract, that makes *YOU* the Prime. As the person in charge, it's up to you to ensure that the work is completed as expected—whether you're the one actually completing it or not.

Subcontractor (aka Sub): A subcontractor (which may be a person or company) is hired by a Prime to help complete the requirements of the contract. A Sub is never an employee, but is instead an independent contractor and is issued a 1099 document at tax time. Think of Subs as team members who contribute to the contract. Often, Primes hire Subs who specialize in the type of work outlined in the contract to complete some, or even all, of the project. Companies of all sizes work with, or can be, Subs. Subs often subcontract some of their work out to other Subs to perform. Therefore, for some contracts, the organizational chart may resemble a Multi-Level Marketing Pyramid (without any fraud)!

Primes may sub out all of the work, or have Subs that sub to another Sub! While there are some limits on the extent of subcontracting, the Prime is held responsible for the contract requirements being met. The rules vary by the type of contract, requirements of the contract, and agency, and are always subject to change, because it's the federal government (cue "I'm just a bill…sitting on Capitol Hill" 🎶 🎼 🎶)!

What Are Small Business Set-Asides?

Importantly, the federal government doesn't just purchase from large companies like Amazon, Boeing, or Lockheed Martin. In fact, it's *required by law* to set aside a certain amount of money to buy from small businesses, like YOU. Remember, 23% of federal government contracts are awarded to small business owners like us. That means those contracts are a tremendous financial opportunity for people like you and me. There's money for the taking, and you deserve your share !

Contracts that are set aside for small businesses are called "set-aside contracts" or just "set-asides." There are two types of set-asides: *competitive set-asides* and *sole-source set-asides.*

Competitive set-aside: This contract type is used when at least two small businesses could supply the goods or services requested in the contract, and therefore there will be a competitive bidding process. With some exceptions, all government contracts under $150,000 automatically become competitive set-asides.

Sole-source set-aside: This contract type is used when the government determines that only one business can fulfill the requirements of the contract. As there's no competition, these contracts are issued without a formal bidding process.

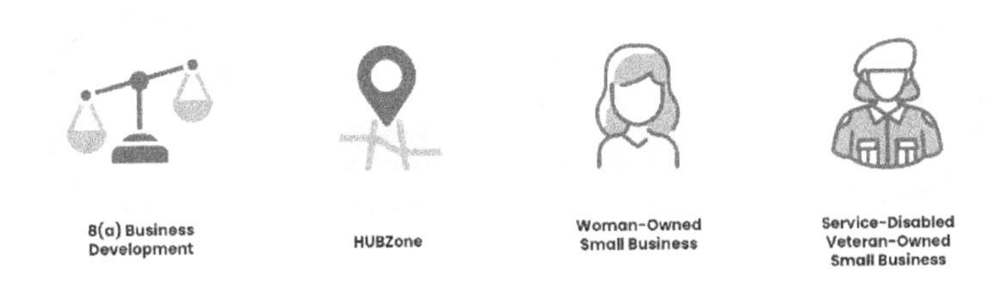

Federal government set-asides: Unique to the federal government are certain specific set-asides based upon socio-economic categories, such as the 8(a), HUBZone, Women-Owned Small Business (WOSB)/Economically Disadvantaged WOSB (ED-WOSB), Service-Disabled Veteran-Owned SB (SDVOSB)/ Veteran-Owned SB (VOSB), Indian-owned and controlled businesses, Alaska Native Corporations (ANCs), and Native Hawaiian Organizations (NHOs) (aka Super 8(a)s).

8(a) Set Aside: The 8(a) Business Development Program is administered by the Small Business Administration (SBA) to help small, disadvantaged businesses compete in the marketplace. It is specifically aimed at businesses that are at least 51% owned and controlled by socially and economically disadvantaged individuals. Selected individuals and their companies may enter this program for up to nine years. It provides benefits including, but not limited to, federal contracting preferences, mentorship, training, and financial assistance. You only get one opportunity to own and operate an 8(a) firm, unless you fall under the Super 8(a) category.

Benefits of the 8(a) Program:

1. **Federal Contracting Preferences**: One of the most significant benefits is the preference given to 8(a)-certified companies when federal contracts are being awarded. The government sets aside a portion of its federal contracts exclusively for businesses in the 8(a) program.

2. **Sole-Source Contracts**: 8(a) firms can receive sole-source contracts.

3. **Joint Ventures and Mentorship**: The program encourages joint ventures with established businesses, which provides 8(a) businesses the experience and mentorship they may lack.

4. **Business Development Assistance**: The program also provides various forms of business development assistance including training, counseling, marketing assistance, and high-level executive development. Each 8(a) firm is assigned a Business Opportunity Specialist, who works for the SBA and provides additional help in these areas.

5. **Technical Assistance**: Firms in the 8(a) program can get advice on how to improve their business, navigate the federal contracting arena, and set achievable targets.

6. **Access to Surplus Government Property and Supplies**: Businesses in the 8(a) program can sometimes purchase surplus government property and supplies at discounted prices, providing cost-saving advantages.

7. **Transition Assistance**: The SBA also offers assistance in transitioning out of the 8(a) program to help businesses continue to succeed after they have graduated from the program.

In short, the 8(a) program aims to level the playing field by giving small, disadvantaged businesses a fair opportunity to compete in a marketplace in which they might otherwise be dominated by larger, more established entities. The end goal is to help these businesses grow to a point where they can compete on their own merits, without the need for special assistance.

As a graduate of the 8(a) program, I can tell you, first hand, that this set-aside is one of the main reasons I was able to grow my team to over 100 people. Today, the federal government can award a sole-source to 8(a) firms in the amount of up to $4.5M. I know a $250k contract would change your life. Now, imagine getting a sole-source contract for $4.5M! You better change, get a second phone, and a good accountant!

Super 8(a)s: Alaska Native Corporations (ANCs), along with other Alaska Native organizations such as tribes, and Native Hawaiian Organizations (NHOs) hold a unique position in the context of the 8(a) program. The 8(a) program also aims to help these small, disadvantaged businesses gain access to federal contracting opportunities, offering a range of support services including mentorship, training, and financial assistance.

Unique Features for ANCs in the 8(a) Program:

1. **Ownership**: While a typical 8(a) company must be 51% or more owned by a socially and economically disadvantaged individual, ANCs can be majority-owned by multiple Alaska Native shareholders, often through a parent corporation.

2. **Size Affiliation Rules**: ANCs are subject to more lenient size affiliation rules. This allows them to form subsidiaries that can individually apply for 8(a) statuses, even if the parent corporation would not qualify as a "small" business under SBA guidelines.

3. **Sole-Source Contracts**: ANCs can receive sole-source federal contracts of up to $100M with the Department of De-

fense (DoD) and $25M for non-DoD contracts with no questions asked, whereas other 8(a) businesses face certain dollar limits on sole-source contracts. This offers significant business opportunities for ANC-affiliated companies.

4. **No Graduation**: Traditional 8(a) businesses "graduate" from the program after nine years and are then no longer eligible for 8(a) benefits. ANC-owned businesses may continue to participate in the 8(a) program beyond the nine years if they meet the requirements, as the ANC itself never graduates from the program.

5. **Community Benefit**: Profits from ANC 8(a) contracting activities are intended to benefit the larger Alaska Native community, including dividends distributed to native shareholders and investments in community programs like education and job training.

6. **Subcontracting**: ANCs have more flexibility in subcontracting than individual 8(a) companies, which can make it easier for them to take on larger or more complex contracts.

Benefits:

1. **Economic Development**: The special provisions for ANCs in the 8(a) program aim to spur economic development in often rural and economically disadvantaged Alaska Native communities.

2. **Contracting Opportunities**: ANCs have a competitive advantage in federal contracting, which can lead to the growth and diversification of the corporation and affiliated entities.

3. **Community Impact**: Through the 8(a) program, ANCs can generate revenues that are then reinvested into community services, education, and other social programs, providing broad-based benefits to Alaska Natives.

4. **Capacity Building**: The 8(a) program helps ANCs build managerial and technical capacity, which can lead to long-term business sustainability.

5. **Networking**: Participation in the program helps open doors for ANCs to partnerships and subcontracting opportunities with larger firms and federal agencies, fostering business growth.

Critics argue that the special privileges accorded to ANCs can lead to abuses or could distort the competitive landscape of federal contracting. However, the unique features of ANCs in the 8(a) program are fundamentally aimed at balancing economic development and community welfare needs in Alaska Native communities.

Native Hawaiian Organizations (NHOs): Having a special status within the 8(a) program similar to ANCs, the 8(a) program is designed to help NHOs gain access to federal contracting opportunities and offers a range of support services, including mentorship, training, and financial assistance.

Unique Features for NHOs in 8(a) Program:

1. **Ownership**: Unlike typical 8(a) companies, which must be 51% or more owned by a socially and economically disad-

vantaged individual, NHOs can own other businesses that participate in the 8(a) program. These businesses may be structured in a way that enables the broader community to share in the benefits.

2. **Community Benefit**: Profits generated by NHO-owned 8(a) businesses must benefit the Native Hawaiian community. This is similar to the community benefit obligations that apply to ANCs in the 8(a) program.

3. **Sole-Source Contracts**: Like ANCs, NHO-owned businesses can be awarded sole-source federal contracts up to $100M with the DoD and $25M for non-DoD contracts with no questions asked, providing them with significant business opportunities.

4. **Size Affiliation Rules**: NHOs have certain flexibilities when it comes to the SBA's size affiliation rules, which enables them to establish and own multiple businesses that can individually qualify for the 8(a) program, even if the parent NHO would not qualify as a "small" business.

5. **Partnerships and Joint Ventures**: NHOs can enter into joint ventures with non-8(a) firms, which allows them to bid on contracts that they may not have the individual capacity to fulfill. This enhances their competitiveness and capacity for larger contracts.

Benefits:

1. **Economic Empowerment**: The unique features for NHOs in the 8(a) program aim to facilitate economic development and empowerment within the Native Hawaiian community.

2. **Federal Contracting Opportunities**: NHO-owned businesses are often more competitive in federal contracting due to their ability to secure sole-source contracts and participate in joint ventures.

3. **Community Development**: Revenue generated through the 8(a) program can be used for community services, education, job training, and other social programs that benefit the Native Hawaiian community.

4. **Business Growth**: Participation in the 8(a) program provides NHO-owned businesses with the training, networking, and resources necessary to grow and sustain their operations in the long term.

5. **Capacity Building**: Through mentorship and training, NHO-owned businesses can enhance their managerial and operational capacities, making them more competitive in both federal and commercial markets.

While the privileges accorded to NHOs in the 8(a) program have been subject to some scrutiny and debate, they are fundamentally aimed at promoting economic and social well-being within the Native Hawaiian community. Like the special 8(a) provisions for ANCs, the NHO provisions seek to balance the need for competitive federal contracting with broader social and economic objectives.

HUBZone Set aside: The Historically Underutilized Business Zones (HUBZone) program is another initiative by the SBA aimed at promoting economic development and employment growth in distressed areas. The program encourages small businesses to either locate in or hire employees from economically disadvantaged areas, specifically designated as HUBZones. You can check to see if your physical location qualifies by checking the HUBZone Map.

The HUBZone Map was recently updated and is used to determine whether your principal office and employees are located in a HUBZone.

To qualify for the HUBZone program, a small business must meet the following criteria:

1. It must be a small business based on the SBA's size standards for its industry.

2. It must be at least 51% owned and controlled by US citizens, a Community Development Corporation, an agricultural cooperative, or an Indian tribe.

3. Its principal office must be located within a "Historically Underutilized Business Zone."

4. At least 35% of its employees must reside in a HUBZone.

Benefits of the HUBZone Program:

1. **Federal Contracting Preferences**: Similar to the 8(a) program, the HUBZone program allows for preference in federal contract awards. Federal agencies aim to allocate a specific percentage of their contracting dollars to HUBZone-certified businesses.

2. **Competitive and Sole Source Contracts**: HUBZone-certified companies can compete for contracts that are set aside specifically for HUBZone businesses. Additionally, they can also be awarded sole-source contracts.

3. **10% Price Evaluation Preference**: In full and open contract competitions, companies in the HUBZone program can get a 10% price evaluation preference, which can provide a competitive edge.

4. **Economic Development**: By encouraging businesses to set up in or hire from economically distressed areas, the program fosters job creation and investments in areas that might otherwise be overlooked.

5. **Reduced Competition**: As these contracts are set-aside specifically for HUBZone businesses, there is inherently less competition for these specific opportunities, making it easier for such companies to win contracts.

6. **Community Development**: Businesses are encouraged to hire locally, which not only brings employment to the community but also circulates money within it, thereby boosting the local economy.

7. **Business Growth and Scalability**: Access to federal contracting opportunities provides HUBZone businesses the revenue and experience to grow, scale, and eventually compete for larger contracts.

8. **Networking Opportunities**: Similar to the 8(a) program, being a part of the HUBZone program allows businesses to network with government agencies and other contractors, fostering relationships that could lead to subcontracting or partnership opportunities.

9. **Enhanced Credibility**: Being a HUBZone-certified business adds credibility to your company. The rigorous certification process can serve as a signal to potential clients and partners that your business is reliable and has met federal standards.

In summary, the HUBZone program offers opportunities for small businesses to gain a foothold in federal contracting while benefiting economically disadvantaged areas. By doing so, it seeks to address the economic disparity in these communities and foster local development and job creation.

Women-Owned Small Business (WOSB): The Women-Owned Small Business (WOSB) Federal Contracting Program is a federal government initiative designed to provide greater access to federal contracting opportunities for women-owned small businesses. Administered by the SBA, the program aims to level the playing field for women entrepreneurs, who historically have had less access to funding, resources, and business opportunities as compared to their male counterparts.

Eligibility Criteria:

To be eligible for the WOSB program, a business must meet the following requirements:

1. Be a "small business" as defined by the SBA's size standards for its industry.

2. Be at least 51% owned and controlled by women who are US citizens.

3. Have women manage the day-to-day operations and also make long-term decisions for the business.

Additionally, there is an Economically Disadvantaged WOSB (EDWOSB) subcategory for businesses that meet certain economic criteria, including limits on the personal income and assets of the women who own them. As of today, very few opportunities are set aside for this designation.

Benefits of the WOSB Program:

1. **Federal Contracting Opportunities**: The federal government has a goal to award at least 5% of all federal contracting dollars to WOSBs each year. Being part of the WOSB program makes a business eligible to compete for these set-aside contracts.

2. **Access to Capital**: The certification can also help when seeking various forms of business financing, as some lenders and investors see WOSB or EDWOSB certification as a positive signal.

3. **Reduced Competition**: Contracts set aside for WOSBs mean reduced competition, increasing the odds of winning a bid. The program allows women-owned businesses to compete more effectively within the federal contracting marketplace.

4. **Networking**: Being certified provides additional opportunities to network with government agencies and prime contractors, potentially leading to subcontracting opportunities or partnerships.

5. **Credibility**: The certification adds credibility to a business. It is often a rigorous process that confirms a business is indeed women-owned and operated, which can be a selling point for certain clients or customers.

6. **Sole-Source Contracts**: Under certain conditions, WOSBs can be awarded sole-source contracts, making the procurement process faster and less competitive

7. **Market Differentiation**: In sectors or industries that are traditionally male-dominated, a WOSB or EDWOSB designation can set a business apart from its competitors.

8. **Publicity and Branding**: Some businesses use their WOSB or EDWOSB status in their marketing materials to attract more customers who prefer to work with women-owned enterprises.

9. **State and Local Benefits**: In addition to federal contracting opportunities, many states and local governments offer similar programs, incentives, or advantages for women-owned

businesses, so the benefits can extend beyond just federal contracts.

You may apply for a WOSB or EDWOSB designation for free on SBA.gov, or use one of the four SBA-approved third-party certification (TPC) organizations:

- El Paso Hispanic Chamber of Commerce
- National Women Business Owners Corporation
- US Women's Chamber of Commerce
- Women's Business Enterprise National Council

The WOSB program aims to address gender disparity in business opportunities and create an ecosystem that is more inclusive and representative. Through providing better access to federal contracting opportunities, the program helps women-owned small businesses grow, succeed, and contribute to the American economy.

Service-Disabled Veteran-Owned Small Business (SDVOSB)/Veteran-Owned SB (VOSB): The federal government provides procurement opportunities to small businesses that are at least 51% owned by one or more service-disabled, or non-service disabled, veterans. This program is designed to support veterans who have served their country and are now transitioning into the civilian workforce as entrepreneurs. Veteran owned firms can apply for this designation FREE on SBA.gov. Certification allows SDVOSBs to compete for federal sole-source and set-aside contracts across the federal government. Also, VOSBs have additional opportunities to pursue sole-source and set-aside contracts at the Department of Veterans Affairs (VA) under the VA's Vets First program.

In order for SDVOSBs or VOSBs to receive a sole-source award from the VA, they must be certified as such by the SBA.

Eligibility Criteria:

To qualify for the SDVOSB or VOSB program, a business must meet the following conditions:

1. Be a "small business" as per the SBA's size standards for its respective industry.

2. Be at least 51% owned by one or more veterans.

3. Management and daily operations must be controlled by one or more veterans rated as service-disabled by the VA for SDVOSB certification.

4. If a veteran is permanently and completely disabled and cannot oversee the day-to-day running of their business, that veteran's company may still be eligible for the program if the veteran's spouse or a designated, long-term caregiver takes on the responsibility of managing the business.

Benefits of the SDVOSB/VOSB Program:

1. **Federal Contracting Preferences**: The federal government sets aside a certain percentage of federal contracting dollars specifically for veterans. The goal is to award at least 3% of all federal contracting dollars to SDVOSBs each year.

2. **Reduced Competition**: Like other set-aside programs, veterans compete against fewer companies for the same set-aside contracts, increasing their odds of winning a bid.

3. **Sole-Source Contracts**: Under certain conditions, veterans can be awarded sole-source contracts, making the procurement process faster and less competitive.

4. **Price Evaluation Preference**: In some instances, veterans may be given a pricing advantage over non-veteran businesses when competing for contracts.

5. **Access to Capital and Business Support**: Specialized loans, grants, and training are often more accessible to veterans, enabling them to kickstart or grow their business more easily.

6. **Networking and Mentorship**: Being part of this program allows businesses to network more efficiently with other veteran entrepreneurs as well as large corporations and government agencies, opening doors to potential partnerships and subcontracting opportunities.

7. **Enhanced Credibility**: The certification process adds a level of credibility, serving as proof that the business is owned by a veteran, which could be a decisive factor for certain clients or customers.

8. **State and Local Opportunities**: Many states and local governments also have veteran programs, providing even more opportunities for contracts and growth.

9. **Social Impact**: The program serves as an avenue for the government and other entities to give back to veterans by providing them with tangible opportunities to grow their businesses.

10. **Market Differentiation**: The SDVOSB/VOSB designation can also serve as a marketing tool, setting a business apart in crowded marketplaces.

Overall, the SDVOSB/VOSB program is aimed at supporting service-disabled veterans and non-service-disabled veterans by providing them with special business opportunities and resources. It rewards their service, helps them in their transition to civilian life, and offers a meaningful way to leverage their skills and expertise in the business world.

Native American Owned (The Buy Indian Act): While not an official set-aside administered by the SBA, the Buy Indian Act was passed in 1910 to provide a preference for the procurement of goods and services from Native American-Owned (The Buy Indian Act) businesses for the needs of the Bureau of Indian Affairs (BIA) and the Indian Health Service (IHS). The act aims to promote economic development in Native American communities by giving preference to Native American producers and suppliers in the awarding of federal contracts. The law is part of a broader effort to encourage the growth and sustainability of Native American-owned businesses and to invest in the economic development of Native American communities.

How to Get Certified: Businesses that are Indian-owned and controlled and wish to bid for set-aside contracts under the Indian Health Service (IHS) Buy Indian Act will need to complete an IHS Indian Economic Enterprise self-certification form. This form will accompany all IHS requests for proposals that are designated under the Buy Indian Act. To submit a bid, the completed and signed form should be included with your proposal in response to the specific IHS request. Once the final regulations are issued and the IHS Indian Health Manual is updated to align with the Buy Indian Act, this form will be accessible on the IHS Division of Acquisition Policy website. For those wanting to get a copy of the form sooner, contact any IHS Contracting Officer. If you have further questions, contact Santiago Almaraz, head of IHS contracting activities, at santiago.almaraz@ihs.gov, or Ken Truesdale, acting director of the Division of Acquisition Policy, at kenneth.truesdale@ihs.-gov.

Why Does the Government Set Aside Money for Small Businesses?

There are several reasons why the government is required to set aside money for small businesses:

1) It ensures that small businesses have a fair chance. Small businesses are important to economic development and job creation, so it's in the government's best interest to make sure they aren't muscled out by larger companies.

2) It gives the government access to new and innovative ideas. Small businesses are often responsible for some of the most important innovations in our society. Most large and successful company that exists today were once small companies with great ideas. Therefore, the government can continue to support and benefit from innovation by setting aside money for small businesses.

3) It provides opportunities to disadvantaged socio-economic groups. Not only does the government set aside money for small businesses, but also for small businesses in certain socio-economic categories, such as WOSBs and SDVOSBs. This ensures that these groups aren't deprived of opportunities and have a fair shot at winning contracts.

So, what does this mean for you? As a small business owner, you can take advantage of these set-asides to win more contracts. Because the government is required to spend a certain amount of money on small and disadvantaged businesses, it's extremely interested in buying from businesses that have those designations.

Basically, it's all about taking the path of least resistance. Just as you like to buy from Amazon because it's fast and convenient, the government likes to buy from the businesses that help them meet its requirements. It's as simple as that!

GovCon Winners™ Mythbusting

Are set-asides your shortcut to an early retirement or to a mansion?

NO. Despite what people in the government contracting space may tell you, set-asides aren't a quick and easy path to getting rich. Just because you qualify to bid on set-aside contracts doesn't mean you're going to be winning left and right. You still need a solid business model and a good marketing strategy to be successful, just as with any other business.

While we're at it, let me be clear that the reverse is also true: You don't *need* to bid on set-aside contracts to be successful in government contracting. As long as you do the work, you can win million-dollar contracts without ever bidding on a set-aside contract.

At the end of the day, set-asides are a means to an end. They can be helpful if you have access to them, but you're not lost without them. The most important thing is that you know your stuff—and incorporate what you learn in this book!

Kizzy Takeaways:

1. The federal government spends over $500 billion annually to work with businesses like yours to purchase products and services, and you, too, can get a slice of this pie.

2. Federal law requires the government to set aside a certain amount of money to buy from small and disadvantaged businesses to ensure they have a fair chance against larger and more powerful companies.

3. Set-asides can give you a competitive advantage in winning contracts, but they're not necessary to win. It's like a hunting license-it means you can hunt, but it doesn't mean deer will just appear at your door!

CHAPTER 2

BUSINESS FUNDAMENTALS

By now, you understand the basics of government contracting—and that's huge! But it's only the first step in the process of learning how to grow a successful business. So stick with me, because there are a few more things we need to cover. If you want to win profitable contracts—and win them consistently—you also need to have a handle on the fundamentals of running a business.

Managing a business centered on government contracting may be a bit different than opening up a restaurant or brick-and-mortar business, but there are still many basic business concepts that apply. You need to understand not only how to operate your business from a legal and logistical standpoint, but also how to develop a strategic business model that can bring in the kind of revenue that will help you get the life of your dreams.

In the following pages, we'll go through all the business basics you'll need to become a successful government contractor. Once you understand these fundamentals, you'll be amazed at just how many contract wins start rolling in.

Legal Considerations

If you haven't yet opened your business, there are some legal considerations you'll need to take into account. Here's what to focus on:

Business Name: Determining a business name is a crucial step in establishing a new venture. The name (♫ ♫ say my name, say my name....) serves as the first impression that government prospects will have of your business. It also plays a role in branding and marketing efforts. Below are some steps and guidelines that might help you determine a suitable business name:

Research and Brainstorming

1. **Understand Your Business**: Make sure you understand your target market, the services/products you'll offer, and the mission and values of your business.

2. **Brainstorm**: Come up with a list of words and phrases that relate to your business. You can involve your friends and family for a broader perspective.

3. **Check Existing Names**: It's crucial to make sure the name you're considering isn't already in use, particularly within your industry. You can check by conducting an internet search as well as a search of the list of existing businesses in your state.

Creativity and Branding

4. **Make It Memorable**: Aim for something easy to spell and easy to remember.

5. **Relevance**: Make sure the name gives at least a clue as to what your business is about, unless you're intentionally going for something abstract (such as "Apple" for a tech company).

6. **Longevity**: Pick a name that will remain relevant even as your business scales or pivots.

7. **Domain Availability**: Check if the corresponding domain name is available, as having a website with the exact business name is beneficial for online presence.

8. **Social Media**: Ensure that the name is also available across key social media platforms for consistency.

Legalities

9. **Trademarks**: You'll want to run a more formal search to make sure you're not infringing on any existing trademarks.

10. **Legal Structure**: Depending on the legal structure of your business (e.g., sole proprietorship, LLC, corporation), there may be specific rules about what your business name can and can't include.

11. **Registration**: Once you've chosen a name, you'll need to register it with the appropriate local, state, and federal agencies.

Testing

12. **Feedback**: Share the name with close contacts to get some feedback. You can also do more formal market testing if you wish.

13. **Say It Out Loud**: Sometimes names look good on paper but sound confusing or are hard to understand when spoken. Make sure to speak the name out loud multiple times to ensure it rolls off the tongue easily.

14. **Local Sensitivities**: If you're planning to do business in multiple regions or countries, ensure your business name doesn't have negative connotations in different languages or cultures.

15. **Future-proof**: Make sure your name can endure and will still make sense if your business expands into different regions or product lines.

You already have a business name: One of my clients had an industry-specific name connected to branding. She was very concerned about it as she was interested in offering middleman services to federal government agencies. She assumed that she would need to register a new business and start over. Thankfully, that was not the case. Instead, she simply created and registered a "Doing Business As" (DBA), also known as a fictitious business name using the initials of her business name. This allowed her to operate the business under a different name than its legal name. This was accomplished by registering the DBA with her state. You can have as many DBAs as your state allows!

By taking the time to consider these factors, you can help ensure that you pick a name that not only fits your business but also stands the test of time.

Business Address: A virtual address which lacks a physical presence, aka a brick-and-mortar building in which you can hold meetings, is not allowed when doing business with the federal government. Instead, a physical address is required, which may be your home or office. You may also use a virtual office, but only if you are issued a lease and/or have access to an office space or conference room in order to conduct business.

Business Banking: Choosing a business bank is a crucial decision that can impact your company's day-to-day operations and long-term financial health. The right bank can provide valuable financial services, resources, and support to help your business grow and succeed. Here are some steps and considerations for choosing a business bank:

Determine Your Business Needs

1. **Type of Accounts**: Decide what types of accounts you need, such as checking, savings, or merchant services (which provides the ability to accept government credit/purchase cards).

Research Banks

1. **Local vs. National Banks**: Local, community banks, and/or credit unions often provide more personalized service, while national banks may offer a broader range of services and more advanced technology.

2. **Online-Only Banks**: Some newer, online-only banks offer competitive interest rates and low fees, but may lack some services such as in-person consultations or a wide ATM network.

3. **Financial Products**: Compare the types of financial products offered, such as interest rates on savings, fees for checking accounts, loan terms, etc.

4. **Reputation**: Check customer reviews, financial stability ratings, and any news stories or reports that might give you an impression of the bank's reputation.

Evaluate Services and Costs

1. **Fees**: Look for any maintenance fees, transaction fees, ATM fees, and other costs associated with the business accounts.

2. **Accessibility**: Consider the convenience of branch locations, hours of operation, and the availability of online and mobile banking services.

3. **Customer Service**: Evaluate the quality of customer service, including the availability of a dedicated business advisor.

4. **Tech Features**: Assess the quality of the bank's digital platform, including ease of online banking, mobile app functionality, and other tech features, such as interoperability with your accounting software.

Personal Preferences

1. **Cultural Fit**: Some businesses prioritize banks that have a culture or mission that aligns with their own values, such as a focus on sustainability or community development.

Make the Move

1. **Visit Branch or Online Application**: Depending on your preference and the bank's process, either visit a branch in person to open an account or complete an online application.

2. **Provide Documentation**: Be prepared to provide necessary documents, such as any licenses, Employer Identification Number (EIN), and identification.

3. **Initial Deposit**: Make your initial deposit as required, and familiarize yourself with the account features and services.

Review Periodically

1. **Periodic Review**: Business needs change, and banking offers do, too. Periodically review your banking relationship to ensure it still meets your business needs.

Selecting the right business bank involves considering a variety of factors, from the basic financial products you need to the level of customer service you desire. Take your time in making this important decision, and consult with financial advisors or other business owners for recommendations.

Legal structure: Deciding on an appropriate legal structure for your business is an essential first step, as it can impact everything from your taxes to what you're liable for. My recommendation is that you structure your business as a Limited Liability Company (LLC), as it has the most advantages for you legally and taxwise. As an LLC, you can select to be taxed as an S-Corporation with the IRS. This means you won't face double taxation, which is when both your business and yourself are both taxed on the same profits. The business will report earnings but won't be taxed on the money it makes, and you will be taxed on the income you distribute to yourself. Also, your personal liability for any company legal troubles is quite minimized-it's right there in the name, LLC. Don't worry, if you later wish to change the form of your business to another legal structure, you can always do that.

Employer Identification Number (EIN): An EIN is necessary for you to file taxes, open bank accounts, and perform other essential tasks. The government requires its contractors to have one. If you don't have one yet, you can get one for free through the IRS. Simply go to IRS.gov for a FREE EIN.

North American Industry Classification System (NAICS): This is a standardized system used in the US to classify businesses into industry-specific categories based on the activities in which they are primarily engaged. The federal government, banks, and most states require each business owner to identify a minimum of one NAICS code for use with each business. You may select as many as you desire and change them. Some popular NAICS codes include:

- 541512 COMPUTER SYSTEMS DESIGN SERVICES

- 541611 ADMINISTRATIVE MANAGEMENT AND GENERAL MANAGEMENT CONSULTING SERVICES

- 561720 JANITORIAL SERVICES

- 561210 FACILITIES SUPPORT SERVICES

- 611430 PROFESSIONAL AND MANAGEMENT DEVELOPMENT TRAINING

Licenses and Permits: Depending on the products and services you intend to offer, you may need to apply for certain licenses or permits to operate legally. The requirements and fees vary based on your business activities, location, and government rules.

Professional Liability Insurance: While it may not be required in your industry or state, it's always a good idea to get professional liability insurance, which can protect you if you're ever sued for negligently performing the services you offer. This type of insurance covers claims such as personal injury, copyright violation, and damages. If your business is in construction or the trades, be sure to carry all licensing, bonding, and insurance documentation required by the jurisdictions regulating your business, as the federal government often asks for this information (or wants proof you have it) before awarding any work.

Workers Compensation Insurance: This is a form of insurance designed to provide wage replacement and medical benefits to employees who are injured or become ill as a result of their job. The insurance is meant to protect both the employee and the employer: the employee receives guaranteed, no-fault coverage for work-related injuries and illnesses, while the employer gains protection against lawsuits related to workplace injuries. This is only needed if you have, or plan on having, employees.

Managing Finances

As a business owner, your goal is to bring in revenue, not spend and accumulate debt. One of the top reasons businesses fail is due to lack of cash flow, and that means you need to have an understanding of how to manage your expenses and make sound financial decisions.

For example, if you're just starting out, you don't need to take out loans from the SBA or spend money on unnecessary stuff like a fancy website, pens, an elaborate office, or advertising. You don't need much to start bidding on contracts—as long as you implement what you learn in this book, you'll start winning profitable contracts in no time!

Business Strategy

Every business needs a strategy to be successful–yes, yours too! If you don't have a proper business model, goals, or plans to achieve them, you'll never get beyond a few chance contract wins. To build a sustainable business you can pass on to your family or sell, you must have a well-designed plan.

While these aren't the only considerations to take into account, here are several things you'll need to think about when deciding on the type of business you want to have—and the success you want to see:

Expert vs. Entrepreneur

There are two paths you can take in government contracting: *expert* and *entrepreneur*. Which path you choose will affect the types of contracts you bid on and the earning potential of your business.

Experts: These are business owners who specialize in a specific area (e.g., resume writing), usually based on their education and experience. They bid only on the contracts related to their specialty, meaning they're able to build strong relationships with agencies that contract within their area of expertise. However, bidding on a limited subset of contracts also means there are fewer opportunities available and less potential for growth.

Entrepreneurs: These are business owners who widen their scope to include contracts related to a variety of products and services (e.g., expanding from IT to HVAC and roofing). They're open to bidding on contracts in many different areas and are willing to find solutions—like hiring Subs and/or practicing the "middleman" approach—so they can take advantage of any existing opportunities. Entrepreneurs are more likely to secure long-term contracts and create ongoing revenue, meaning they have the potential to build multimillion-dollar businesses.

Both paths are viable options. I know contractors who have built successful businesses as experts and entrepreneurs. You just need to understand the growth potential of each path and develop a strategy that makes sense for that type of business.

Low-Risk vs. Medium Risk Products and Services

In addition to choosing between the expert and entrepreneur paths, you'll also need to decide which types of products and services you plan to provide. Certain products and services are valued more highly than others and will therefore create more competition, but also the potential for more revenue.

Low-Risk: Low-risk products and services are perceived by the federal government to involve a minimal likelihood of negative outcomes, loss, or harmful consequences. In other words, serious consequences won't occur if someone messes up. Which you'd never do because you are a GovCon Winner and reading my book!

If you plan to bid on contracts for low-risk products and services (e.g., landscaping, roofing, electronics, paving), you're going to face a high level of competition because those areas are saturated.

Those contracts will also usually (but not always) be worth less money because the government doesn't value something like janitorial services as highly as graphic design. That means you'll need to bid on (and win) a large volume of contracts to make an income. For example, the National Oceanic Atmospheric Administration (NOAA), Solicitation Number NWWX1000-2300209KAW, has a requirement for Janitorial Services at two locations, one in Miami, FL, and the other in College Park, MD. NOAA has a contract with the incumbent (aka, the company which won the work) for $57,240.00, covering janitorial services over the course of five years. Say the incumbent is making a profit of $200 a month on this work. That's not enough to retire on or leave a full-time job. Instead, to increase revenue, you'd need to win 50 janitorial contracts to potentially bring in a profit of $10,000 a month. Of course, the profit will vary depending on the size and frequency of the janitorial contract. Nonetheless, volume is required to make this line of work profitable.

Medium Risk: On the other hand, "medium risk" is used to describe products and services perceived by the federal government, where the likelihood of negative or harmful outcomes falls between low and high-risk scenarios. In a medium-risk situation, there are moderate chances of experiencing adverse results, but also reasonable opportunities for benefits or rewards. In other words, there is the potential of a negative outcome if a company doesn't perform, but it wouldn't be catastrophic.

While bidding on contracts for medium-risk products and services (e.g., research, technology, engineering) may seem intimidating and require more effort, it will also result in a bigger payoff. There's far less competition for these types of contracts, and if you win, you have the potential to earn hundreds of thousands—or even millions—in revenue and/or profit. Get this, while there are hundreds of thousands of firms registered to do business with the federal government, on average no more than five companies submit for the same bid. It's amazing, most go through the process to become registered on SAM.gov and do nothing. Similar to a gym membership, one gets it and never uses it.

Once again, it's entirely up to you to decide which types of contracts you want to bid on. However, you should consider what makes the most sense for your business. Experts often automatically bid on medium/high-risk contracts, because they tend to specialize in areas that are viewed as more valuable or professional. Plus, since there are fewer options available, they *need* to win contracts that are worth more money in order to sustain their businesses.

Entrepreneurs have more options, but that doesn't mean they should forgo strategy. Bidding on a lot of low-risk contracts can certainly sustain your business, but volume is needed if you want to be able to afford that all-inclusive vacation to the Bahamas or send your kids to private school.

One-and-Done vs. Multiyear Contracts

Contract length is another aspect to consider when developing your business model. Like low-risk and medium-risk contracts, the length of the contracts you aim for will impact not only the amount of energy you spend on bidding, but also your earning potential. So, it's important you understand the difference between *one-and-done* and *multiyear* contracts.

One-and-done: This type of contract has a one-project duration and typically last less than one year. It lasts only as long as you need to fulfill what's requested, whether that's painting a building, moving furniture, or analyzing a collection of data. There's no continuity to this type of contract: once it's finished, your paid relationship with the agency comes to an end.

Multiyear: This type of contract (aka "Base-Plus") is a commitment by the government to purchase products or services from you for more than a year, and often up to five or 10 years. The benefit to multiyear contracts is that you're able to build an ongoing relationship with an agency and create a reliable income stream for your business.

Think of it this way: Why do businesses like Amazon push subscription services? Because it allows them to bring in consistent revenue! They don't have to rely as much on your neighbor purchasing an airfryer or smartwatch if they know they're getting monthly payments from *you*. It's the same in government contracting—securing a multiyear contract is like getting the government to buy your subscription. It gets a reliable product or service, and you get consistent money in your pocket.

Middleman

The term "middleman strategy" in the context of federal government contracting typically refers to the use of intermediaries or brokers who act as go-betweens for the parties: the contracting agency and the contractor actually providing the goods or services. This strategy is most commonly seen in subcontracting or teaming arrangements, where a Prime serves as the "middleman" between the agency and various Subs.

Here's how the "middleman" strategy may work:

Roles and Functions:

1. **Prime Contractor**: These are the firms that actually win the federal government contracts. They have the primary relationship with the federal government and are responsible for the overall delivery of the project.

2. **Subcontractors**: These are specialists or service providers hired by the prime contractor to perform specific parts of the contract. They have a contractual relationship with the prime contractor, not directly with the government.

3. **Teaming Partners**: These are other companies that may join forces with the prime contractor to bid on a contract, bringing specialized skills, certifications, or resources to the table.

Strategy:

1. **Specialization**: Often, no single company has the expertise or resources to fulfill every aspect of a large federal contract. Subcontractors or teaming partners with specialized skills are therefore needed.

2. **Compliance and Risk Mitigation**: The prime contractor is responsible for ensuring that all work complies with federal regulations, including the work done by subcontractors. Acting as a middleman allows the prime contractor to oversee compliance and manage risks more effectively.

3. **Set-Asides and Preferences**: Sometimes, federal contracts are "set aside" for specific types of businesses, such as minority-

owned, women-owned, or veteran-owned businesses. A larger prime contractor might partner with these smaller businesses as subcontractors to meet these set-aside requirements.

4. **Scale and Efficiency**: By serving as the central coordinating entity, the prime contractor can achieve economies of scale and operational efficiencies that individual subcontractors may not be able to achieve on their own.

Benefits:

1. **Streamlined Communication**: With a middleman in place, the government has a single point of contact, which can make contract management more straightforward.

2. **Quality Control**: The prime contractor has a vested interest in ensuring that subcontractors meet all the quality and compliance requirements set forth by the government contract.

Challenges:

1. **Markup Costs**: Using a middleman often means added costs, as the prime contractor will typically mark up the costs of subcontracted work to cover their overhead and profit margins.

2. **Complexity**: Managing multiple subcontractors can introduce complexity and potential delays, especially if there is poor coordination.

Understanding the roles and strategies associated with being a "middleman" in federal government contracting is crucial for companies looking to enter this sector, either as a prime contractor or as a subcontractor. It involves specific responsibilities, including compliance with various regulations and effective coordination among all parties involved.

Marketing

Just because you have a good product or service doesn't mean people have heard of you or will do business with you. To be successful, you need to know how to market your business so you can show people what you have to offer and persuade them to buy it.

Take restaurants, for example. They could have the most incredible food in the world, but if they don't entice you to come try it with mouth-watering photos and hard-to-resist promotions, you may never know it exists.

We'll dive further into marketing later, but for now, just understand that there's more to running your business than having something to offer—you have to show agencies why they should work with *you* rather than someone else.

Managing Relationships

Even if you're a solopreneur, running a business isn't a solo endeavor. Whether interacting with contracting agents, small business advisors, subcontractors, vendors, or the people you meet while networking, it's essential you know how to conduct yourself with professionalism—that includes being on time, dressing appropriately, and holding yourself accountable, among many other things.

It's also a good idea to develop your negotiation and selling skills. Whether giving a capability brief to a contracting agent or working with a vendor, being able to negotiate, persuade, and tell a story is key to building longevity in government contracting.

Making a *GovCon Winner*: Matt

To help you understand the importance of these business fundamentals, let me share an example from my experience mentoring Matt.

Matt reached out to me on Instagram, which is something that happens to me quite a lot. While I appreciate when people connect with me, I often have to filter these requests with qualifying questions to know whether the person is really serious about working with me.

So, I asked Matt whether he already had a CAGE code (more on that later) and had paid for coaching in the past. He immediately responded that he had a code and had, in fact, worked with a coach, which told me he was at a point where I could potentially offer him some help.

We connected over the phone shortly after, and Matt filled me in on his journey thus far. He was a super entrepreneurial-minded individual who was clearly passionate about government contracting and all the opportunities it could provide him. He had already given up everything out East and moved down South for this new start in government contracting.

Despite his enthusiasm, Matt wasn't winning contracts consistently—maybe a 25:1 ratio of losses to wins. He knew he was missing something, but didn't know exactly what it was. That's why he had reached out to me.

Fortunately, I was able to identify right away what was going on: Matt was missing some key business basics that he needed in order for his contracting business to take off. Specifically, he hadn't developed a functional business model, and was only bidding on low-value contracts that would never help him achieve his financial goals.

After filling Matt in on some of the information covered in this chapter, the transformation was immediate. He ended up winning a five-year contract providing debris removal and now has a publicly traded company subcontracting to him.

Kizzy Takeaways:

1. Finding success in government contracting requires an understanding of the basics of how to run a business. Without that, you may win contracts, but not nearly enough to achieve the life you've always dreamed of.

2. As a government contractor, you can choose the path of an *expert*, who bids on contracts related to their specialty, or an *entrepreneur*, who looks for opportunities regardless of the area. No matter which path you choose, understand your growth potential and develop a strategy that aligns with that model.

3. The government doesn't value all products and services equally. To face less competition and make larger amounts of money, you'll need to bid on contracts related to high-value industries, such as tech or graphic design.

4. To bring in consistent revenue and obtain financial security for your business, aim to win multiyear contracts, where the government commits to contracting with you for as many as five to ten years.

CHAPTER 3

THE GOVCON WINNERS™ APPROACH

So far, we've covered the basics of government contracting and the fundamentals of running a government contracting small business, which is a solid foundation! Before you can go out and start winning contracts consistently, however, you need to know how to find them in the first place.

Opportunities—or prospects—don't just appear out of thin air. As with any business, you have to invest time in lead generation, or the process of attracting prospects to your business and increasing their interest in working with you. Without putting in the time to market your business, you won't have any contracts to bid on!

When it comes to finding contracts or creating opportunities for your business, there are four different ways to go about it. Together, they make up the *GovCon Winners™* Approach. While you don't have to use all of the strategies to be successful, it's a good idea to use some combination of them, as each one has its advantages and disadvantages.

In this chapter, we'll take a closer look at each of the strategies and how to implement them effectively. With this knowledge, you'll be well on your way to growing a successful business through government contracting!

Strategy #1: Searching Online and Bidding

The easiest way to start finding contracts is to search for existing opportunities online. It's the approach most often used by beginners because it's the most 'hands-off' strategy. Go online, search for contract opportunities, and bid on those that make sense for your business. In many ways, it's like going on Upwork or Fiverr to bid on freelance gigs.

The most common place to search for contract opportunities is SAM.gov (System for Award Management). It's the official, primary website of the US Government to post available government contracts. There are also other government websites you should search, including:

- DIBBS (DLA Internet Bid Board System)
- Unison
- GSA's AAAP (Automated Advanced Acquisition Platform)
- GSA's RSAP (Requirement Specific Acquisition Platform)
- GPO (Government Publishing Office)
- FedConnect

Recognizing a Good Opportunity from a Bad One

Once you're registered on SAM.gov, you can start bidding on as many contracts as your heart desires, with one important caveat: not every contract opportunity is a *good* opportunity! Think of it like foraging in the woods—you don't want to end up eating something poisonous just because it looked like a big, juicy berry.

Understanding what a solid opportunity looks like is key to winning contracts online. To avoid eating poisonous fruit, you need to pay attention to several details:

- **Set-Asides:** Notice which set-asides are listed. You can only bid on the opportunity if you have the type of set-aside the agency requires. Only search for Total Small Business Set Asides (TSBSAs) or partial small business set asides on SAM.gov if you hold another set-aside, such as a WOSB, SDVOSB, etc. Most of you reading this book are small business owners like me. Now is the time to take advantage of those set-asides. This way, you are decreasing your competition and not competing with firms like SpaceX, Amazon, and Lockheed Martin for those contracts.

- **Types of Opportunity:** Sources Sought Notice (SSN), Request For Information, (RFI), Request for Quote (RFQ), and Request for Proposal (RFP) are terms commonly used in the federal government procurement and contracting process. Each serves a different purpose and is used at different stages of the procurement cycle. Here's a breakdown:

SSN (Sources Sought Notice)

A Sources Sought Notice (SSN) is a request issued by a buying organization (often a government agency) to determine the availability and capability of potential business sources to meet a particular project or procurement need. SSNs are *not* solicitations for work, but are instead market research tools used to identify qualified businesses that can fulfill specific requirements. By responding to an SSN, businesses get the opportunity to present their capabilities and possibly influence the final requirements of a forthcoming solicitation.

What It Is: A preliminary notice issued by a buying organization to determine the availability and capabilities of potential suppliers. It's a market research tool rather than a solicitation for work.

Purpose: To identify qualified businesses capable of fulfilling specific project or contract requirements.

Typical Use Case: Early-stage market research to help refine the scope and specifications of a future procurement action.

RFI (Request for Information)

A Request for Information (RFI) is a formal request issued by a buying organization to collect written information about the capabilities of various suppliers. Much like an SSN, an RFI is usually a preliminary step and doesn't guarantee that a contract will be awarded. It serves as a tool for gathering information to help make informed decisions. RFIs are generally followed by more specific procurement actions, such as a Request for Proposal (RFP).

What It Is: A formal request for gathering written information about the capabilities of various suppliers.

Purpose: To collect data and insights that will inform future procurement decisions. It doesn't guarantee a subsequent contract.

Typical Use Case: Market research, especially when the buying organization is considering a future procurement but hasn't yet defined all the details or specifications.

RFQ (Request for Quotation)

A Request for Quotation (RFQ) is a formal request issued by a buying organization for the submission of price quotations or bids for a specific product or service. Unlike a Request for Proposal (RFP), which often requires a detailed plan for how the supplier will meet project requirements, an RFQ is generally used when the specifications of a product or service are already known and price is the main, or only, factor in selecting the successful bidder.

What It Is: A formal request for suppliers to provide a price quote for specific goods or services.

Purpose: To gather pricing information, usually when the specifications of the product or service are already well-defined.

Typical Use Case: Procuring standardized, off-the-shelf products or services where price is the primary concern.

RFP (Request for Proposal) / Solicitation

A Request for Proposal (RFP), or Solicitation, is a formal document issued by a buying organization inviting suppliers to submit proposals to provide specific goods or services. Unlike an RFI or an SSN, an RFP contains detailed specifications and requirements for the goods or services needed. Suppliers respond to the RFP with a detailed proposal explaining how they will meet the requirements, at what cost, and within what timeframe. The buying organization then evaluates the proposals and selects a supplier based on various criteria such as cost, capability, and the quality of the proposal.

What It Is: A formal document inviting suppliers to submit a proposal for a project, specifying detailed requirements and criteria.

Purpose: To collect comprehensive proposals for fulfilling specific project requirements, including technical specifications, timelines, and cost estimates.

Typical Use Case: Complex projects where various factors (e.g., technical capability, experience, price) will influence the buying decision.

Key Differences:

Complexity: RFPs are generally the most complex, followed by RFIs, RFQs, and then SSNs.

Stage of Procurement: SSNs and RFIs are usually early-stage tools used for market research. RFQs and RFPs are used later when the organization is closer to making a buying decision.

Focus: SSNs and RFIs focus on capabilities and general information. RFQs focus on price, and RFPs focus on comprehensive solutions, including technical approach and cost.

Commitment Level: RFPs and RFQs are used for actual procurement and usually require a more detailed response, while SSNs and RFIs are more preliminary and less binding.

Why are they used?

SSN: Used for preliminary market research to identify capable vendors and refine the requirements for a potential contract.

RFI: Also used for market research but typically collects more detailed information than an SSN to inform future procurement actions.

RFQ/RFP/Solicitation: Used when the buying organization is ready to procure and wants to compare price or detailed proposals from various suppliers.

Each of these tools plays a specific role in the procurement process, helping organizations make informed, competitive, and effective buying decisions.

- **Deadline:** Pay attention to the submission deadline. I practice the rule of 10. I rarely bid on any opportunity in which there are fewer than 10 days between when the notice was originally released and the deadline for responses. Typically, a shorter deadline means the opportunity has been 'tailored' for another business. No worries, because soon, opportunities will be tailored for you, too!

- **Evaluation Criteria:** The attachments, acronyms, and more may seem overwhelming. They were for me for a long time, too! I didn't learn this secret until later in the game, and I don't want you to go through years of not winning because you didn't know this either: in about 99% of federal government opportunities posted online, the "Evaluation Criteria," "Basis of Award," or other ways of saying this, are listed. Immediately look for these, read them, and accept them. For example, if the evaluation criteria is "Lowest Cost Technically Acceptable," this is what I would call a low-risk opportunity, and agencies will make an award based solely upon pricing. If you are fine with that, then bid. If, however, the evaluation criteria is "Past Performance," defined as, say, three completed past performance questionnaires with resumes to be provided for your team, and you can meet this requirement, then bid. If not, pass it up, regardless of whether you can do the work.

As I noted, it's also in your best interest to be mindful of contract opportunities that could be "tailored" for someone else. This means that the evaluation criteria in the opportunity are so narrowly established that it seems only the person or company that an agency has already determined that it really wants can meet those criteria and get the contract. Although you could bid on these (and lose), and then file a bid protest and follow those procedures, you probably don't want to waste your time bidding on a contract whose lucky (or not-so-lucky) winner is already set, and which agency doesn't want to work with you, anyway.

It is NEVER about whether you can do the work! The secret is, CAN YOU **WIN** THE WORK? You will ALWAYS be able to do the work or to find someone to do it. I know this because I did, and you will too!

- **Bidding, or Writing the Proposal:** Every proposal your write will differ based upon the evaluation criteria, requirements, and level of complexity of the work. Most low-risk opportunities may simply require pricing and an 'about us' section, while high-risk opportunities may require three volumes and past performance questionnaires. To best address this topic, I've provided an overview on how to write a proposal.

Proposal Matrix: This is a tool that may be used in the process of preparing a proposal and can be a Word or Excel document. The matrix serves as an organizational framework to help in mapping and keeping track of various elements of the proposal. These elements should include any requirements from the RFP/RFQ/Solicitation, evaluation criteria, guidelines, tasks to be performed, deliverables, team responsibilities, timelines, and such other mandates from the agency.

Basic Components of a Proposal Matrix:

1. **Requirements**: List all the specifications, evaluation criteria, conditions, and requirements set forth by the client in the RFP/RFQ/Solicitation.

2. **Response/Approach**: Next to each requirement, detail your approach or solution to meeting that specific criterion.

3. **Responsible Team Member**: Indicate who within your team is responsible for each task or component.

4. **Resources Needed**: Identify what resources (e.g., time, budget, materials) will be required for each task.

5. **Timeline**: Establish a timeframe for when each task or requirement will be completed.

6. **Page/Section Reference**: Once the proposal is drafted, use this column to indicate where in the proposal document each requirement can be found.

Benefits of Using a Proposal Matrix:

1. **Organization**: A proposal matrix helps to organize your thoughts, ideas, and solutions in one place, making it easier to write a cohesive and comprehensive proposal.

2. **Team Alignment**: A matrix helps you align team members with their respective responsibilities and tasks, ensuring that everyone knows what parts they play in the proposal process.

3. **Quality Control**: By cross-referencing the requirements with your response on the matrix, you can ensure that all client needs and queries are addressed, thereby improving the quality of your proposal.

4. **Efficiency**: Using a matrix can speed up the proposal preparation process by eliminating redundancy and helping to identify gaps or overlooked requirements.

5. **Compliance**: A well-structured proposal matrix makes it easier to check that you have adhered to all guidelines and requirements, reducing the risk of disqualification for non-compliance.

6. **Strategic Focus**: The matrix can also help you identify the most critical aspects of a proposal where you may need to focus your most persuasive arguments or most robust solutions.

Creating and using a proposal matrix can significantly improve the proposal development process, helping teams to produce more compelling, organized, and successful proposals.

The Actual Proposal: For most opportunities located on Unison, GPO.gov, and DIBBS, which are product related or low-risk such as janitorial services, the actual proposal is simple. They typically want a price quote, proof of insurance, an acknowledgement of the country of origin for the product, and perhaps samples, if applicable. As for other opportunities located on Unison or SAM.gov, they typically desire more information, which is why creating a proposal matrix is KEY when responding to bids.

For all non-product related proposals or medium to high risk opportunities, I submit the following as a minimum:

- Cover page
- Cover letter
- Signed SF 1449
- Signed Amendments (as applicable)
- Copy of our Reps and Certs/FAR & DFARS Reports. Don't worry, this seems daunting, but these are available on SAM.gov once you obtain a CAGE (Commercial and Government Entity) Code.
- Company Profile ('About Us' information)
- Any additional requirements as identified in the Proposal Matrix
- Pricing

How to Submit: Follow the requirements in your Proposal Matrix. Typically, all of this information should be saved as a PDF. If pricing is requested to be sent in an Excel file, then this is saved as an Excel document. The PDF and Excel are then emailed to the agency Points of Contact (POCs), and acknowledgment of receipt of the emailed submission requested.

Then, we typically email and/or call those POCs within three weeks to learn where they are in the evaluation process. Do not call or email them too often as you don't want to annoy them. You may call them more often if you have a relationship with them.

Expect to learn the outcome of the contract award within 30 days. The agency may call or email you. It is important that your voicemail isn't full, you are prepared to call back any strange numbers, that your email account is functioning, and that you are checking it daily.

One of my coaching students was contacted on a Saturday with the good news and was asked to sign the contract asap. Remember, the federal government is open 24 hours a day!

GovCon Winners™ Mythbusting

Do you need marketing materials like a website or Capability Statement to win contracts?

No. A lot of newbies think they need to invest a bunch of money into creating a fancy new website to get contracts, but in reality, you don't need any marketing materials at all to build a successful business through government contracting. The strategies I discussed above are more than enough to help you win your first federal government contract!

You *can* use a website as a sort of landing page that lets connections learn more about your business. By publishing your capability statement, case studies, white papers, and more on your existing website, you can quickly show people everything they need to know about what you bring to the table.

There are also other online strategies you can leverage for more marketing power that are even more effective than having a website. LinkedIn, for example, is a great way to make connections with agency representatives and other business owners. Also, speaking at virtual conferences, hosting webinars, or even conducting Facebook Live events are great ways to get your name out there and draw attention to your business.

Strategy #2: "Dialing for Dollars"

Finding existing opportunities is great, and profitable! To take things to the next level, however, by minimizing competition and creating your own ocean to grow a long-term profitable government contracting business comes down to playing the long game. This means creating *future* opportunities by establishing connections with contracting agencies. You can do this through what I like to call "dialing for dollars," or cold calling.

The benefit of marketing your business to agencies is that it gives you the opportunity to build a relationship that can cut through the competition. Like regular people, agency staff are more likely to work with business people they know, like, and trust—plain and simple. So, the more contact points you have with them, the more likely they are to want to contract with you, as long as you're increasing their value.

Deciding Who to Dial

Before you start reaching out to agencies left and right, think about which ones actually make the most sense to target. This isn't about casting the widest net possible. After all, dialing for dollars isn't a one-and-done type of deal. Making connections with agencies requires a lot of time, patience, and persistence. So, you should be strategic about who you contact—because you're going to be doing it *a lot!*

Here are some of the things you should consider when deciding which agencies to dial:

- Which type of agency do you want to target?

- Which agencies do you already know?
- Which agencies already have opportunities posted online?
- Which agencies tend to buy what you sell?

Once you've established your parameters, you can find the contact information of different agencies by going to www.acquisition.gov. Depending upon the agency, you'll be reaching out to either their small business representative or industry liaison. If possible, it's often better to talk to small business representatives, because their objective is to help small business owners like us win contracts, and are usually quite eager to help us!

Example Scripts-Use for Both Emails and Phone Calls

Sample Cold email/phone script for the Small Business Professional

Subject line - {Your Business Name} {Designations to your business like: 8(a), EDWOSB, etc.} {CAGE Code}

Good morning {Name of Small Business Specialist},

Please allow us to introduce ourselves.

{Your Business Name} {Designations to your business like: 8(a), EDWOSB, etc.} {CAGE Code}

{Description of your business' main services. How long you've been serving the government. Any agencies you've worked for or are currently working with.}

{Anything that makes your business stand out from the competition.}

I am attaching our Capability Statement {Your Business Name} so that you can become familiar with us.

Would you kindly provide a link to the forecast of contracting opportunities? And, if you are able to provide any leads or advice that would, also, be greatly appreciated.

If you are available, we respectfully request a Capabilities Brief between yourself and {Name of person that Capabilities Brief is to be done with} {Job Title of person}.

{Your Name}
{Your Job Title}
{Your Phone Number}
{Your Email}
{Your Business Name}
{Your Business' Address}

{Your Business' Website or LinkedIn}

Sample Cold email/phone Follow up script for the Small Business Professional

Subject line - Company Name and CAGE Code

Good afternoon XXXXXXXX,

We previously sent our Capability Statement to introduce ourselves. Are you available to do a Capabilities Brief with XXXX, President of XXXXX?

Sincerely,
{Name}
{Title}
{Website (or LinkedIn)}
Phone number}

Sample Cold email/phone Follow up 2 script for the Small Business Professional

Subject line - {Your Business Name} {Designations to your business like: 8(a), EDWOSB, etc.} {CAGE Code}

Good afternoon {Name of Small Business Specialist},

We know your schedule is busy.

If there is any way you can squeeze {First Name of Person Capabilities Brief is to be with} in for a Capabilities Brief next week, we would be very grateful.

Thank you!

{Your Name}

{Your Job Title}
{Your Phone Number}
{Your Email}

{Your Business Name}
{Your Business' Address}
{Your Business' Website}

Persistence Pays Off

Dialing for dollars is all about playing the long game. Whether you're reaching out to a contracting officer or small business representative, they're not likely to want to make time for you right away. So, to secure a meeting, you're going to need to be persistent.

The goal is to create as many points of contact as possible, which means you should aim to contact them in any way you can: phone, email, LinkedIn, or any avenues available. You should also plan to reach out to them through each of those channels at least once a week (yes, you read that right!) until you get a meeting with them. If you do that, eventually someone is going to bite!

Remember: These agencies aren't out there looking for you. As a small business, it's up to *you* to go out and market yourself so that they can understand all the value you can provide!

Conducting Capability Briefs

Eventually, all that persistence will pay off, and you'll succeed in securing a meeting with a contracting agency. It's a big win, and you deserve to celebrate! However, it's neither the final step nor the most important one. Meetings are your one and only chance to show agencies what you're capable of and why they should work with you instead of someone else.

During the meeting, you'll conduct what's called a *Capability Briefing*. A Capability Brief is an opportunity for the agency to get to know you and you to get to know them. Much like a job interview, the questions go both ways, as both parties want to make sure that there's something of value to be gained by working together. So, it's a good idea to prepare some questions beforehand, such as:

- "Do you do business with new government contractors?"

- “What suggestions do you have for new businesses”

- “Do you hold in-person or virtual events? If so, may I be added to your email list?”

The Brief may last anywhere from 15 minutes to an hour, and during that time, you'll present your *Capability Statement*. The Statement, or "one-pager," is a document that outlines your expertise and what makes you stand out from other businesses.

Importantly, the point of the Brief isn't to highlight how long you've been in business or the number of awards you've won (you can place that information in your Statement!). It's about positioning yourself as their *solution* through proof of what you've done, as well as the value you can offer.

If you have a special certification, technology, or patent that sets you apart, make sure to let them know. If you've worked with a client in the past, walk them through the situation-action-result of the project. And if you haven't, no worries. You don't necessarily need experience to get their attention. Talk about what you or your business bring to the table in other ways.

At the end of the day, your job is to craft a story about you and your business that leaves the agency POCs convinced that *you* are the person for the job when the opportunities arise.

Following Up

If you thought your days calling and emailing were over, think again. Once you've met with an agency representative, it's more important than ever to follow up with them. You want to ensure the great impression you just made doesn't fade into the background. Don't be afraid to be the squeaky wheel to get that grease!

At a minimum, you should follow up immediately after the meeting to thank them for their time and reiterate your interest in working together in the future. It's also a good idea to reach out every once in a while to update them on the goings-on of your business. Letting them know about the successful completion of further projects, new certifications or patents, or your latest product or service offerings not only keeps them updated on the value you bring to their agency, but also keeps your business at the forefront of their minds.

> **Subject:** Thank You for the Capability Briefing Opportunity
>
> Dear [Recipient's Name],
>
> I wanted to extend my heartfelt appreciation for you taking the time to attend our Capability Briefing earlier today. Your attention, and the insightful questions posed by the [Agency/Organization Name] team, truly demonstrated your commitment to finding the best

solutions for [Specific Goal/Need, e.g., "enhancing IT security across federal agencies"].

We value the opportunity to discuss how [Your Company Name] can potentially serve [Agency/Organization Name] in the future. I hope our presentation clearly communicated our expertise and dedication to [Specific Task/Area, e.g., "providing top-tier cybersecurity solutions"].

If there are any additional questions or if you require further details regarding any aspect of our briefing, please don't hesitate to contact us. We are more than willing to provide any necessary follow up information.

We look forward to the possibility of collaborating with [Agency/Organization Name] and appreciate your consideration of our capabilities. Thank you once again for your time and attention.

Warm regards,
[Your Name]
[Your Job Title]
[Your Company Name]
[Contact Information, e.g., Phone Number, Email]

Strategy #3: Networking

In addition to reaching out to agencies directly, you can also build relationships and increase the likelihood of future contract opportunities by simply being in the right place at the right time. By that, I mean going to the places where contracting officers and small business representatives hang out and networking to establish connections.

There are a ton of different networking opportunities that you can take advantage of as a small business owner, including:

- Outreach events
- 1:1 matchmaking events (where you're paired with an agency)
- Vendor days
- Exhibits
- Industry days
- Business development associations

Take advantage of any opportunities you may have to speak at live events. While going as an attendee is still a great way to network, speaking is an easy way to set you apart from the crowd, get your name out there, and let people know about your business.

Networking Tips

A lot of networking comes down to navigating the complexities of human relationships. But there are also many different strategies you can use to ensure that you get noticed and make the most of your interactions:

- **Believe in what you sell:** If you don't, no one will want to partner or buy from you! You must have the confidence of Beyoncé and Coach Prime! I don't know about you, but I don't buy from people or companies who don't believe in what they sell. You are amazing, or else you wouldn't be reading this book. Believe in what you sell and show it! As the business owner, YOU are the best sales person for it, because the federal government is buying because of you.

- **Show off your set-asides:** As mentioned, agencies are looking to work with small businesses that have set-asides. So, you can get noticed and spur conversations by making that information readily available. One way to do this is with color-coded ribbons on name badges (like red for women-owned businesses).

- **Carry copies of your Business Cards and Capability Statement:** Be prepared to market your business at any given opportunity by carrying copies of your Statement. Placing QR codes on your business cards and Statements makes it easy for agency reps to learn about you.

- **Attend educational sessions:** When events include educational sessions, make sure you're there. It's important to get information and network with other attendees.

- **Be coachable:** Especially when you're first starting out, many people you meet will have a lot of wisdom to share about government contracting and business ownership. Taking their advice is not only beneficial to you, but also shows *them* that you're open to learning and collaborating—a good indicator of what it's like to work with you.

- **Get intel:** Networking isn't just about talking about your business—it's also a good chance to learn about opportunities and get tips and tricks from those with more experience than you. Your goal in every conversation should be to get as much intel as you can.

Kizzy Strategy: Get Those Numbers!

As any marketer will tell you, any opportunity you can get to speak directly to your prospects is the best way to convert them into customers. In the government contracting space, that means getting the cell phone numbers of contracting officers, small business representatives, or other business owners.

When you're networking at events, don't leave any conversation without exchanging contact information—especially phone numbers. Going through the trouble of establishing connections with the people you meet won't do you any good if you can't continue that relationship.

Within 48 hours of the event, make sure that you call, text, and/or email the people you've met to set up a Capability Brief and send them your Capability Statement. After that, follow up at least once per month. Remember, persistence is key!

Strategy #4: Finding Partnerships

The final strategy you can use to find contract opportunities is to establish partnerships with other businesses. The benefit of working alongside other companies as a subcontractor is that it opens you up to opportunities that wouldn't have otherwise been available going at it alone (not to mention it saves you from having to do the actual bidding yourself). If all goes well, partnerships can lead to exciting future opportunities, such as joint ventures.

Partnerships are often a natural byproduct of using the other strategies, but they can also be an approach to getting contracts in their own right. There are a few different ways they usually come about:

- **You search for opportunities online:** Like looking for contract opportunities on SAM.gov, you can also search for partnerships by browsing the government's prime contractor directory, looking on LinkedIn, the SBA Dynamic Small Business Search, and of course in my Facebook Group. In addition, you can reach out to companies in your area or network and let them know you're on the market and interested in freelancing.

- **You find opportunities through networking:** Networking can lead to all sorts of opportunities, including partnerships. You never know who you're going to meet and what they may be looking for, so keep yourself open to whatever types of collaborative projects come your way.

- **A prime contractor reaches out to you:** Sometimes, prime contractors with the intention of bidding on a contract will reach out to other businesses who could help them with the project. For example, I was recently approached by a Prime looking for companies that have done training for the DoD. That's why it's important that you market your business—you never know who may be interested in what you have to offer!

You can prepare for conversations with potential partners by having an arsenal of key questions to ask, such as:

- Are you seeking another contractor?
- What kind of contractor/partner are you looking for?
- Do you have past performance or a relationship with the buyer?
- What areas of capability are you looking to build up?
- Do you currently work with other contractors or 1099s?

No matter how you happen upon opportunities, the key to partnerships is ensuring that your business adds something of real value. For me, that is my set-asides, past performance and contract vehicles. My experience can give other business owners a lot more value, which makes a partnership with me much more enticing. The same applies to you!

The bottom line is this: As long as the Prime has something the government is seeking, and you can contribute something meaningful to their bid, they'll be interested in partnering with you.

Kizzy Strategy: Sign an NDA

Anytime you start getting into negotiations with another small business, you should absolutely, positively conclude a Non-Disclosure Agreement (NDA). An NDA is a legal contract that's meant to facilitate confidentiality between two parties. Essentially, it obligates both businesses to keep certain information confidential.

You need NDAs to protect your business. When you partner with another company, you may need to share information—such as ideas or trade secrets—that you don't want others to know about. By obliging that the business you intend to partner with keeps things confidential, you're preventing important information from being shared or exploited.

If you're looking for help in creating an NDA, *GovCon Winners™* has a free bundle that includes templates for an NDA, teaming agreement, and work breakdown.

Kizzy Takeaways:

1. According to the *GovCon Winners*™ Approach, there are four different ways you can find contract opportunities: searching online, dialing for dollars (cold calling), networking, and establishing partnerships with other small businesses.

2. When it comes to contacting agencies, persistence is key. Aim to create as many points of contact as possible (e.g, phone, email) and plan to reach out to them through each of those channels at least once a week until they agree to have a meeting.

3. Capability Briefings and Statements are musts, whether you brief during a scheduled meeting with an agency or give to the people you meet while networking. These allow you to succinctly demonstrate what you bring to the table and showcase what sets you apart from other businesses.

4. Establishing partnerships with other small businesses is a great way to open yourself up to contract opportunities—make sure you and your partners sign NDAs! Often, you can find partnerships online or happen upon them through networking. It's also possible to sign on as a Sub with a business looking for someone who can help them fulfill a contract.

CHAPTER 4

BUILDING RELATIONSHIPS

You're now familiar with the four different ways you can find contracts: searching online, "dialing for dollars," networking, and finding partnerships. Used together, these strategies will help you gain access to opportunities that could lead to BIG wins for your business and move you one step closer to the life you dream of.

Yet, as we touched on in the previous chapter, the journey from searching for opportunities to actually winning those contracts involves a lot more than just showing up and parading your awards and set-asides around. You have to dedicate time and effort to building relationships with people.

Because this concept is absolutely vital to your success in government contracting, I want to spend some more time explaining exactly *why* building those relationships is so important, how to do it effectively, and how creating these connections can lead to incredible opportunities for your business—now and in the future.

Why Relationship Building Works

There are many reasons why relationship building helps you win contracts, but at the center of all of them is the idea that people are more likely to buy from someone they know, like, and trust. If you can check those boxes, you'll be well on your way to success in government contracting.

If we want to get specific (and we do!), relationship building works because it helps you accomplish several important things at once. Let's take a look at each one so you'll understand just how powerful creating these connections is for your business.

Reason #1: It Provides an Opportunity to Demonstrate Your Value

The government is filled with people who are no different than you or me—they want to solve their problems, too. And just as you wouldn't buy a product you didn't believe in, neither would they. Just as we talked about in Chapter 3, to win contracts, you have to prove to agencies that *you* have the solution they're looking for, and relationship building is how you do it.

You can more easily demonstrate the value your business brings by fostering genuine connections with the people you talk to. It's not about scheming and schmoozing—it's about telling stories, asking questions, actively listening, and trying to understand their needs. When you do that, the knowing, liking, and trusting come easily.

When they know, like, and trust you, they'll be more likely to consider you a viable option. Or, at the very least, they'll be more willing to listen to what you have to say. At the end of the day, you can leverage the good rapport that you have built with people to influence their decision making when the time comes.

Reason #2: It Gives You a Competitive Edge

No matter which contracts you go after, there's always going to be some competition. If you have your eyes set on those high-value, money-making contracts, you're going to eventually compete with businesses that are bigger and more well-known than yours.

To stand a chance against the big guns, you're going to need to do more than just brag about your experience and try to sell stuff. That may work for companies like Amazon and IBM, but it's not going to work for you. Fortunately, relationship building can help you stand your ground when the bigger businesses try to muscle you out of the way. When the people at the government agencies know, like, and trust you, they are more likely to choose *you* over others.

Reason #3: It Helps You Overcome Biases

People are biased, and the government is run by people. That means—you guessed it—the government is biased, too. While you may not be able to change the way people think, you *can* give yourself a leg up by understanding how their brains work and playing by those rules.

Agencies want to work with businesses they see as capable (remember, they want solutions)! Unfortunately, a small business they've never heard of (with potentially limited experience) is not going to give the impression that it knows what it's doing—at least not at first! But, by building relationships that get them to know, like, and trust you, you can overcome those biases and show them you're the right person for the job.

Reason #4: It Creates Long-Term Partnerships

You won't get far in government contracting if you're only focused on 'the now.' Sure, you can jump from contract to contract, thinking only of the step in front of you. That kind of mindset, however, won't lead to the long-term opportunities that will get you that luxury house you've always dreamed of. To have a shot at those contracts, you need to create long-term partnerships with agencies that lead to multiple or multiyear contracts.

Relationship building is the key to making that happen. When agencies know, like, and trust you, they don't just want to work with you once—they want to work with you *always*. Think of it like that mechanic you've been seeing for years. When your car breaks down, that is the *only* mechanic you trust to get the job done right. It's the same in government contracting. When you have a great relationship with an agency, they'll want to hire *you* when they have a project.

Case Study: The Power of Second Money

My coaching client Tony's first contract was for a concrete slab effort with a federal government agency. He subcontracted the work while project managing everything. All along the way, he practiced relationship building with the agency staff and with the subcontractor to ensure that he always over-delivered. Once the project ended, he practiced the 'GovCon Winners Second Money Technique,' in which he asked the agency staff if they had any additional work or similar efforts at their other locations. This paid off, and the contracting officer directed him to a current opportunity in SAM.gov. He is currently responding to that opportunity and has a high likelihood of winning, as he had fostered a relationship with the agency staff.

All It Takes Is One

It's important to remember that all it takes is one good relationship to start you on the road to success. You don't have to get every single agency to know, like, and trust you—and in fact, you *can't* get every agency to be your 'number one fan.' Establishing a relationship with just one agency is the foot in the door you need to access all kinds of future opportunities. So, focus your energy on the prospects that look promising and let go of the rest.

Kizzy Strategy: The More Obscure, the Less Competition

All you need is one agency, and if you really want to increase your odds, aim to build relationships with other agencies that are more obscure. Why? Because there's far less competition, which will make it easier to make contacts and foster connections.

For example, everyone wants to contract with the Army or Navy, so your chances of establishing any kind of relationship there are rather slim. If you go for the lesser known Department of Interior, however, you have a much better shot at getting your foot in the door, because if you've never heard of them, it's likely other businesses haven't, either.

Navigating Relationships

So, we've established that relationship building works—but that doesn't mean creating connections is automatic! Just as with all relationships, you have to know how to navigate them to avoid problems and keep them going strong. While this is a topic that could warrant its own book, there are a few things I want to mention that you should keep in mind.

Boundaries are Key

Boundaries are incredibly important—not just setting them, but defining what they are in the first place. When you have a good understanding of what you're okay with and what you're not, you'll have an easier time building relationships with people.

Take flirting, for example. For me, I don't bat an eyelash when someone comes on to me—it's just part of the game. But for others, that may be a deal breaker. Know your limits and stick to them, and you'll avoid mishaps that can threaten relationships.

Similarities Sell

People prefer others who are like them. It's a scientific fact. That means that when you're building relationships with people, the quickest way to get them to know, like, and trust you is to find ways to highlight your similarities. So, rather than talk solely about you and your business, ask them questions so you can find out more about who they are. That way, you can identify overlapping interests and opinions and bring them to the forefront.

Kizzy Takeaways:

1. Relationship building works because people are more likely to work with someone they know, like, and trust.

2. There are a lot of powerful benefits to building relationships. Creating connections with agencies can provide an opportunity to demonstrate your value, give you a competitive edge, help you overcome biases, and create long-term partnerships.

3. When it comes to navigating relationships in the government contracting space, it's important to identify and stick to your personal boundaries. Knowing what you're okay with and what you aren't can make building relationships easier.

4. You should also keep in mind that psychology plays a big role in relationships. Similarities and dissimilarities among people *will* affect how they approach and receive you, and people are naturally drawn to others who are like them.

CHAPTER 5

STEP INTO SUCCESS

So far, you've learned the basics of government contracting and how to run a government contracting business. You've also learned the different ways to find contract opportunities and how essential building relationships is to your success. Now, it's time to take action!

It may be hard for you to believe, but you already have everything you need to get started in government contracting. You were ready before you even read this book (although what you've learned will definitely make it a heck of a lot easier)!

As I mentioned at the beginning, if there's *one* thing I want you to take away from everything we've talked about, it's that *anyone* can become a government contractor. There may be a lot of moving parts and critical strategies to master that will help you build a more successful business, but the important thing is to *just get started.* Commit to putting one foot in front of the other, and you'll be amazed by where you end up.

The good news is you've already taken the first step toward success: reading this book!

Step #1: Done!

My intention in writing this book wasn't just to give you practical advice on how to get started in government contracting. It was also to help you develop the mindset you need to be successful. My hope is that everything you've learned will give you the confidence and drive to go out there and get your hard-earned money back from Uncle Sam.

The following steps in your journey are all about taking that winning mindset and fundamental knowledge and putting them into practice.

Step #2: Register Your Business

The very next thing you're going to want to do is legally register your business. Whether as an LLC or another structure, the important things are that you register with a *physical address and register with your respective state*. I can't tell you how important this is. Connecting your business to a physical place—even if it's your home address—is non-negotiable.

If your business is already registered, make sure you pay the annual registration fees to your respective state, maintain all business licenses (including with your state, county, and city), and store all business records.

Step #3: Purchase a Domain

You may not need a website to have a government contracting business, but you *do* need a domain name—aka the *address* for a website. It's a must-have for any small business because it lets you have control over your online presence—whether you intend on investing time in a website or not.

But it's more than that. A domain name also helps you establish authority by allowing you to create an official business email. This is crucial for building credibility with contracting agencies, as a professional-looking address makes you look like you know what you're doing, and some agencies actually require it.

Also, if you *do* decide you want to build out a website for your business, you already have the domain.

Step #4: Register with SAM.gov

As discussed in this book, searching for contracts online is one of the easiest ways to find opportunities, and SAM.gov is the most common place to do it. That means it's the *first* place you'll want to go to get started in government contracting. That said, it's not exactly the easiest website to navigate, so you may need some guidance to get it set up properly.

Here's what you need to do:

1. Register your business information under "entity registration."

- You'll need a copy of the IRS form that lists your EIN, as well as all supporting documentation (such as your business licenses) that demonstrate you have a legal business and physical location.

- You'll also need your business bank account information and your NAICS codes on hand. Only one NAICS is needed; you can update these once your CAGE code has been issued. *If you don't have a business bank account, you can use a personal account and simply update it once your CAGE code has been issued.*

- Then, you'll need to make sure you enter the spelling of your business name *exactly* as it appears on your IRS form.

2. After filling in the necessary information, you'll need to wait a few weeks for the government to issue you a Unique Entity Identifier (UEI).

   - Be sure to check for updates periodically in the "workspace" area.

3. With your UEI in hand, the final step is to get a CAGE code.

   - At this point, the government will ask for additional documentation to validate your business and physical address.

Go Out and Make It Happen

Once you've taken these steps and obtained a CAGE code, you can finally bid on contract opportunities and start to make your dreams a reality. The world is *yours,* and I have every confidence that you can and *will* be successful, because #EverythingisPossible!

To give you an advantage, here are some things I recommend you do. They're easy, 100% free, and can make a big difference for your business as you're getting started:

1. Subscribe to the *GovCon Winners*™ YouTube channel, where we post new educational videos every week.

2. Join the *GovCon Winners*™ Facebook Group, where you can connect with other people who are building businesses in government contracting.

3. Go to SBA.gov and register for one of their contracting assistance programs, which are designed to help small businesses win a fair share of government contracts.

4. Register for an APEX Accelerators program (previously called PTACs) to get the education and training businesses need to become capable of participating in the DoD and other government contracts.

5. Vote! The government has a say about many of the aspects related to government contracting and your business, so make sure your voice is heard.

GovCon Winners™ Mythbusting

Is my success really dependent on who's president?

Technically speaking, your success as a government contractor isn't dependent on who's president. I've managed to build an incredibly successful business through several presidential administrations. However, the person in charge *does* affect what the government is interested in buying and where they buy it.

Typically, democratic presidents have been more minority and small-business supportive, but not always. For example, President Biden supports awarding government contracts to businesses that haven't yet received one through the "Creating a More Diverse and Resilient Federal Marketplace through Increased Participation of New and Recent Entrants" effort. On the other hand, republican presidents tend to emphasize the usage of government employees, big businesses, and "large small businesses," aka those making over $30M or so a year. Therefore, to continue getting business under a conservative administration, it's best you align yourself with a large business and/or Native Alaskan or Hawaiian companies.

The bottom line is that politics *do* impact your business in some way. The best thing you can do to ensure that business continues as usual is to vote to elect the administration you support—and that supports you! If you cannot vote, do what's needed to support your desired candidate(s). Either way, politics and cash rule everything around us 🎶 🎶 🎶.

Kizzy Takeaways:

1. *Anyone* can start a business in government contracting. As long as you put in the work, keep a winning mindset, and apply what you've learned in this book, you can become just as successful as I have.

2. Make sure to register your business with a physical address, purchase a domain, and create an official business email address. These steps will ensure that the government sees you as a credible business.

3. When registering with SAM.gov, you'll need to have all your important documents in order to avoid delays in having your business verified. Once you receive your UEI, you can finally get your CAGE code, which is the last step before you can bid on contract opportunities.

4. There are many free and easy steps you can take to give yourself an advantage as a beginning government contractor, including subscribing to our *GovCon Winners*™ Youtube Channel and Facebook Group.

5. I have a ton of valuable real-world experience in winning government contracts, which makes me an extremely valuable resource for anyone looking to take their business to the next level. Working with *GovCon Winners*™ is the surest way to achieve success and build the life of your dreams.

Take Your Business to the Next Level with *GovCon Winners™*

Speaking from personal experience, success will come if you follow what I've taught you in this book—but it will come a lot faster if you have someone to guide you on your journey.

And that someone can (and should) be me!

Since I started in 2008, I've been awarded over $50M in federal government contracts. I've helped everyday people like you win over $10M in government contracts in under 12 months, and their stories are shared in the next chapter.

With me as your guide, you can avoid time-consuming mistakes, master the same strategies that have helped me build my success, help others win government contracts, and streamline your government contracting trajectory.

Are you ready to take it to the next level?

Become a Part of GovCon Winners™ by going to www.govcon-winners.com and signing up for the waitlist!

CHAPTER 6

SUCCESS STORIES–INTERVIEW STYLE

In the sprawling, complicated world of business, there exists an arena that is both challenging and rewarding: government contracting. The stakes are high, competition fierce, and rules, at times, labyrinthine. Yet, amidst the complexity, there are tales of businesses that not only navigated these choppy waters but also rose to unparalleled heights, setting benchmarks for others to follow.

The realm of government contracting is not just about securing bids; it's about realizing visions, fueling growth, and contributing significantly to national projects and public services. Behind each contract win, there's a story—of grit, strategy, relationships, and sometimes, serendipity.

This chapter introduces you to a series of such stories, a curated collection of success tales that inspire and inform. The stories ahead serve as both a beacon and a roadmap. Whether you're a fledgling enterprise seeking a foothold or a seasoned player looking to scale new heights, these narratives offer invaluable lessons, reminding you that success in GovCon, as in life, often comes to those who dare to dream and have the determination to realize those dreams!

$100k in less than 12 months - Anna Ricks

Kizzy:

Anna Ricks is Director of Operations for Donnell & Company, LLC, and recently won, in under a year, a contract worth $127,000. I'm so excited to welcome Anna. Welcome.

Anna:

Thank you, Kizzy. I appreciate it.

Kizzy:

I appreciate you. Talk to us, because first and foremost, how did you get into government contracting? What do you sell? Tell us about this contract. Everybody's going to want to know.

Anna:

Okay. Our CEO, Kevin Williams, started everything. He kicked everything off, laid the foundation. He is an Army vet, and after 24 years, he retired. And in doing so, he went into business for himself. Then he brought me on board. Right before I retired from the Air Force after 22 years, he asked if I wanted to go into business with him when I retired. And I was like, "Yeah, sure." It was uncharted territory so I was a little bit nervous.

After I retired, we went into business and we started government contracting. It was the challenge for him that he wanted. And he said, "If it's easy, everybody will be doing it." That's one of the things that got us into government contracting.

Kizzy:

If I recall, you first started out selling products, which a lot of people think, 'oh, I'm going to sell a ton of products and retire on that yacht or something.'

Anna:

Absolutely. He is very good with building relationships. With him talking, that's his game, not mine so much. I lack in that area. But with him, he can get in the door, and then the next thing you know, things start to happen. Yes, we got a few six figure supplies with DoD and other agencies out there. And that's what started, I guess, the energy in order to get more and want more, and just the hunger for it.

Kizzy:

Which is great because it's what's needed. I firmly believe it's easy to win a contract, but the challenge is getting more and more work and figuring out what type of work. You were selling, I feel like it was not helicopter parts, but it was some extreme parts. We're not talking pens and pencils.

Anna:

Yes, all of that, Kizzy. Went from styrofoam plates and knives and packets in order to assist with some operations, and then it went to a plane! I was like, "I got to find a plane. What?" And then it went to a part for a ship. It was crazy. He's talking to all these people, and they're like, "Okay. If you can find it." And his thing is, call us and we'll find it. Whatever you have, it's nothing that we can't find. Yes, they call him, "Hey, we need a plane." "Okay."

Kizzy:

Well, I think this is amazing. And I hope people are picking up this because you didn't talk about his background being in aviation. And that's the beauty of government contracting is that as long as you can source it, you can win the opportunity.

Anna:

Absolutely. And it is interesting you said that because his background is IT, and my background is criminal justice, so that's what we're working with right now.

Kizzy:

That is wild!

Anna:

It really is!

Kizzy:

And it shows you don't have to have this background that people think (you do). It's helpful that you're both veterans. And thank you both for your service.

Anna:

It's an honor to serve.

Kizzy:

The business is Service-Disabled, an SDVOSB.

Anna:

Yes.

Kizzy:

And what have you found when it comes to that? Has it been helpful? Was the process easy as far as getting it?

Anna:

The process was a little...it had its bumps, but it wasn't as bad as we thought it would be in order to get the SDVOSB and the many other credentials that we do have. It wasn't hard. And you know what? It might not have been hard because I didn't do it. But he took care of all that; laid the foundation for the entire company. It's been easier for me to step in and just do the things that need to be done in order to get us across the finish line.

Kizzy:

Which is great. You're a director of operations; that's vital. And so how did you go from planes and parts for ships and plastic wear to janitorial? How did you make that leap over to services?

Anna:

Early on in 2022, the goal was made to get a services contract. And (we) wanted to go into the VA system. I don't know if you remember this.

Kizzy:

I do.

Anna:

He was huge on VA.

Kizzy:

Huge.

Anna:

He was like, "I need a VA contract. I want a VA...." This is when we met you. This was it. And I'm pretty sure you were looking at my face like, okay, because I was nervous. But he wanted a VA contract. And most of the ones that we would see had something to do with janitorial work, and so that's where he felt as though that was our avenue. That was our foot in the door to get janitorial with the VA.

Went to a few site visits. And there's a lot of red tape, as you would say. And there was a lot of work put into it. With us not having that background, we took a step back, and we were like, "Okay, let's find something a little bit smaller that we can manage a little bit better," and then we can work ourselves up to that, to where we have the clientele or the subcontractors in line in order to do those things. Yep, services were just added to the books in order to give another line of some type of credit onto our resume.

Kizzy:

And I want to commend the two of you because we've been working together for a year, and what I want to point out is that you were okay with pivoting.

Anna:

Yes.

Kizzy:

Because often we come in and it's like, "This is what we're going to sell," or, "This is what we sold before, so we want to do it again." And there's nothing wrong with that. It's amazing to sell planes and parts, or to want to sell IT, or even going on these site visits, but then to just take it all in and say, "Hold up, hold up. I'm going to pause, we're going to put a little pause here, in order to figure out what are some better fitting efforts to win, which is key because that's going to lead to a long-term and more stable business than just going out and winning." And then it turns into, "Oh my gosh, Kizzy, we won, but, how do I fund this $28M contract? I have to pay $13,000 for mailboxes." These are real things that come up that people have recently DM'd me about, and there are a ton of financing companies, but it's also being aware of that so that when you win, then the win doesn't become a burden. You want every win to be a blessing.

Anna:

Absolutely. And pivot is my favorite word. I love to add it. I was like, "Oh, that's it." Yes, because we're in the military, especially for my job, I always had to adapt or pivot in the blink of an eye. So, being able to do this was a natural step for me, even though it was scary. It still is scary. Every day is a different journey, but I'm trying to overcome that fear. And that's where I feel like you helped out a lot because it took me a long time in order to be able to talk to people and not feel as though I'm asking them. Selling myself was hard for me. It was hard, hard, hard. And I was so unmotivated, and I got to a point where I was like, "Do I really want to do this?" And you say, "It happens to everybody," and it happened to me. But something happened, I did my pushups, and next thing you know I was in the door like, "Hey, how y'all doing?"

Kizzy:

Yes, I love that because, first and foremost, you're always a pleasure to talk to from day one.

Anna:

Thank you.

Kizzy:

You're so kind, you're so sweet. So when it comes to connecting with an agency, I'm not worried, and if I'm ever worried, usually, I would never coach that person.

Anna:

Really?

Kizzy:

Yeah, because I'm not a community college. I'm Harvard over here. I don't take everybody. And so because what's vital is client relations, and if the person comes off like Clear Pepsi, then the government's going to think of them the same way. It's going to be hard unless they have somebody there, unless they have somebody else on their team who's the person that engages with the government, and then they're just a silent owner. I really haven't come across that except for more advanced companies, meaning that they've been in business for several years and they may have an owner and they run operations or they're doing finance. And then you have the other owner who's all about shaking hands, kissing babies, and all of that.

So, yeah, you're amazing at it and I'm so glad that you stuck with it because you ended up with this janitorial win. So talk to us about janitorial, because you know I'm not a huge fan of janitorial, but I'm going to say this, you have helped change my mind at least about it. I'm being serious. I was, with a circle strikethrough, "No janitorial." So, talk to us about this win because this is tremendous.

Anna:

I remember bringing it to you, and actually that meeting you were like, "Hey, I heard y'all got some janitorial stuff. Let's talk about it." And I was like, "Oh, here we go. Here we go." So I'm pacing the floor as we're on. My camera's off and I'm pacing the floor. I'm like, "Okay. She is about to hit me hard, hard, hard, hard, and I'm going to have to really think about what we're doing." So, I found this one. We're in San Antonio right now so I wanted to make sure that what I found was in the area so that I could actually see it, manage it, be in the area, those types of things. I found one that's close by and went to the site visit, and I printed out all my information. I had the floor plan, I had the numbers, I knew who all the contracting officers were, and was on time, just being myself.

And as I told you, I said I looked at everybody in the face like, "I'm going to win this one." And walked in, we went over the site. We did everything, walked through all the rooms, talked about everything. I'm taking pictures. Other individuals that were there at the site visit were asking questions that I was answering. And the contracting officer was like, "Oh, you did your homework." So, just trying to stand out in front of those individuals and spark a little bit of fear into them and to gain a little bit of trust with the contracting officers. It's a five year (contract) and it is one day out of the week, and we usually go in on Sundays in order to do just floors. It's about 24,000 square feet of floor work only. No restrooms. No any of that. Just straight floor.

Kizzy:

Yes.

Anna:

Yes, straight floor. So I thought it was perfect for us, as a leader. Do you want me to go into how the whole contract went?

Kizzy:

Share whatever you're sharing. I just want to add what I love about this and what I want people to know, when it comes to janitorial work or other work where it's once a week, it's once a month, it's once a quarter, you will need volume. It's just how it is. Because we're the same way. If you were to pay for cleaning services, I pay for cleaning services, and I get them twice a month. I'm not going to pay somebody $100,000 a year for cleaning, because there's just no reason to do it, so I want people to realize that. So, this is a huge blessing because it's setting them up to easily win a bunch of additional janitorial work. Please share more about it!

Anna:

After the site visit, I called the contracting officer and I asked about their question and answer (period), when did it end, and if there were any opportunities for me to ask some questions about the contract? And after that, they were like, "Yes, you can go ahead and submit it." I submitted my questions, my key questions...such as, "Who's the incumbent and what was the last bid?" So, I asked those questions, and they gave it up. It was maybe a day before the award. Well, before the closeout, they gave up who the incumbent was. I saw who the incumbent was, got the numbers, and this is when we were at the meeting. Remember, you went in and you were like, "Who is this person?"

Kizzy:

I went in hard, but, thankfully, Lori Davis, my Director of

Getting Things Done, I feel like she was the saving grace, because she was like, "This is amazing." And I think you even talked to her, too.

Anna:

Yes. When we found out we got the award, I called you. We called you first, then we called Lori. We were like, "Somebody has to pick up. She needs to know that we won. Oh, my gosh." And it was on Kevin's birthday, so it was awesome. It was awesome. It just couldn't have come at a better time. And it was the end of my deadline because I had a little deadline, a goal. That was the last day that I needed to get something rolling, and it happened.

Kizzy:

And you manifested this, too, let me say. During the site visit, she's like, "I looked everybody in the eye. I wanted them to know I'm going to win." You came prepared.

Anna:

I did.

Kizzy:

You not only came prepared, but it came off with you answering the questions, with you having the documents there. All of these things, the government takes notice, just like us. How many times have we seen some repair truck or van drive by and it looks crazy and we think like, "Ooh, we don't want them to do anything in our house or in our yard"? And so this is the equivalent to that, by showing up, being early, being prepared, because then she already stood out. And then to follow up with the questions is key, because then you knew what was going on. Because, I remember, during the coaching, you had mentioned the building hadn't been cleaned since May. So, it also showed something was up. There's something going on so they clearly want someone who is going to be competent and not, "Oh, I heard online I can win these contracts. I'm just going to win some janitorial work," and then they're back to square one and the building's still dirty. Nobody wants that.

Anna:

Exactly. I was taking in every little bit of information that I could get. I was on intel like, "Okay, so it hasn't been done then, so maybe they'll be flexible in their pricing. They weren't satisfied with the work so maybe if I show some initiative, they'll know that I'm there for a reason and I'm there to do a good job."

Kizzy:

Yes. And that's why, also, if possible, it's in your best interest to go to the site visit, if it's possible, because no one can sell the business like we can do so. And you did so by being there, because when it's outsourced, and, again, you gotta do what works best for you. I'm not asking anybody to get in debt to travel all over the country to go to site visits. But, just keep in mind when you ask someone to represent you, you have to keep in mind that you don't know what you're going to get.

I went to one site visit with somebody I was coaching, and it was for roofing. And what I found really interesting was the number of people who left the site visit early. And I thought, well, what if one of these companies was called by somebody, and they're like, "Oh yeah, I went." And I'm like, you didn't even stay for the whole site visit. You came in, you went out. I'm like, "There's multiple roofs to look at". You had to go up ladders and stuff. I was like, this is intense.

So what is next for you?

Anna:

Next? So next, I believe that we're going to go into a few more supplies and then dive into other services as soon as we have this one buckled down. Want to make sure this is buckled down and we've got the rhythm and everything's good to go with it. And I know it's the end of the fiscal year. So starting out the next year, get some supplies in, and then look for those services that we can maintain.

Kizzy:

And where do you normally search for the different supply opportunities?

Anna:

All over for supplies. For supplies-

Kizzy:

Unison.

Anna:

Oh, Unison, so Unison is not my friend, but we've had our ups and downs on Unison. If the opportunity is there, I'll do it. It just depends. But SAM.gov is huge. And then we've been looking into some local areas from Dallas to here in order to make sure that we're getting, I guess the max for our time and effort.

Kizzy:

And what would you say to people who were kind of like you a year ago, who maybe they served or they maybe have sold a couple things, and they're like, "Hey, I really want to go and expand in the government contracting space." What would you recommend that they look into doing?

Anna:

I would say that it is worth it. It's worth your time. It's worth the effort. It is an adrenaline rush. And you are going to get so much out of it professionally and for just building your wealth as an entrepreneur. It is so worth it. I would not have done anything differently. And all of the things that I did go through, the ebbs and flows, I do feel like that they were for a reason. I've learned from my mistakes and I've been able to capitalize on those things. With the coaching that we've gotten from you and all the resources that we get, I can always tap into it if I think it's something that's different, or I can go in and... look and I'm like, "oh, we had a call on that." Or, we have something that just jogs my memory a little bit, and I'm able to follow those guidelines in order to get where I need to be. Not saying that I'm a huge expert, but I feel like I have all the tools that I need in order to be successful.

Kizzy:

And what you've done is you are executing. That's what's key. And you've won. The fact that you have a CAGE code and you won contracts before we met, but you continue to win contracts... and then you pivot it into services, that's huge. There are many, many people out there who maybe they've won something. I get messages all the time, "Hey, I won an opportunity. I've been on 50, I haven't won since then." Or, "Hey, I subcontracted. I didn't even realize it was a government contract." That's always the most intriguing. And they're like, "Now I want to do more of this."

And there are tons of companies who rush to get a CAGE code, rush to get set asides, and then they rush to no contracts because there is a process that applies. And so I commend you because it's about learning, and you put it into action. Because you didn't have to go to that site visit, you didn't have to come prepared. You could have just been on your phone. You could have been like, okay, whatever. But no, you didn't do that. And that's one of the main reasons that you won, because that personal interaction is so key if you can do it.

Anna:

But, I do want to say thank you for the tough love. I'll say the tough love, remember when I couldn't find the scope of work or the evaluation criteria.

Kizzy:

Oh, yes.

Anna:

Yeah, yeah. I was like, oh, she's mad at me.

Kizzy:

I wasn't mad!

Anna:

But, it was in order for me to be able to find it and to see what the evaluation criteria is, and if I could do it. And now if I look at solicitations, I find it quick. I'm on it. I'm good to go. And I really do appreciate that, everything. It was needed. That's what I need. I need that extra little, especially coming out of being retired and thinking, is this really worth it? And yeah, I needed that. And it helped out a lot. It was on both sides. Kevin was on this side and you were on this side. He's like, "Is that what she needs?" Then that's what you're giving, tough love.

Kizzy:

Love Kevin. He's awesome. Yeah, and it's a big piece because no one is going to do it for you. Now I mean, if somebody wants to pay six figures, okay, potentially, and there may even be people out there with, "hey, I can get you a contract." Okay, interesting. So what's important is being able to know how to fish.

And that's why I really harp on finding the evaluation criteria because it's in about 90-95% of all federal opportunities. They tell you how they're going to make the decision, and that's the best way to then decide, is it worth the work? Because if they would've made the decision based on, and they sometimes do this, where they'll ask for a resume or the experience of the people who are doing, providing the cleaning, and they'll ask for some interesting things. And for some, hey, I have no problem, I'll do that. For others, it may be that I don't want to do all of that. But, you at least get to make the decision because now you know that's of importance to them, where you may have a similar cleaning contract for a different agency and they could care less. And all they care about is the money. How much are you going to charge them?

But again, you have to know because then that's how you make those smart business decisions. So, I commend you on not giving up, because there were lots of people I would push back and then I haven't heard from them. But that's life, right? That's life. 20% usually go forward, whatever it is, whatever it is. It could be in sales, it could be in athletics, it could be in marriage, it could be love. And when I say go forward, I mean implementing what they're being taught, whatever the topic is. So, you're in a rare group. You and Kevin, you both are.

Anna:

We're trying.

Kizzy:

No, you're doing more than trying. You're crushing it. I'm so proud of you. I'm so, so proud of you.

Anna:

The only thing that I would say is that you're going to, like I said before, you're going to be nervous. You're going to get some unmotivated times, and you're going to fear failure. No one that knows me, especially in the military, would ever say that I was fearful of anything, but this, yeah, every day I did not want to face it because I feared the failure part of it. You're going to get a lot of nos. But that yes, it is that thing. The nos are okay, but it just prepares you for that yes. And when you get that yes, it is the best thing ever. And you're going to be happy that you got some of those nos because some of them weren't even worth it. It was just practice.

Kizzy:

I love that. And what's meant for you is meant for you. And so I love that. And I love your positive attitude. That's also why you're going to keep excelling. You have that light, you have that positivity. So keep going out there. Keep going to site visits. Keep being the outward person, because you have nowhere to go but up, up, up, and more up.

Anna:

Thank you. You and your team. Awesome. Thank you for just allowing us an opportunity to be in front of you and everybody…there's not a greater group of individuals that I would rather take this journey with than GovCon Winners!

7 Figure Win: With No Past Performance - Steve Dixie

Steve Dixie:

I got an email saying, "Hey, we won't accept your bid." It was in the seven figures, easy. Didn't know anything about the margins, a lot of nos. It wasn't overnight. You can go to these state agencies and find something like that. This program, he did a contract within eight to 12 weeks. There were times that I was like, man, I don't know if this is going to work.

Dr. Kizzy Parks:

I'm so excited to introduce you to Steve Dixie with Gateway Integrated Solutions. He is a GovCon Winner and I'm so, so excited to learn about his contract win. Talk to us about who you are, what you do, and how did you get into this space?

Steve Dixie:

Just a quick, high level background of myself. I'm retired military, spent 20 years in the Air Force. Spent a lot of time in the paralegal legal field. Once I retired, I worked in corporate America, working at FedEx headquarters in Memphis, Tennessee. I worked at International Paper in Memphis, Tennessee, always being a paralegal and then an HR paralegal. Moved from Memphis back to Richmond, where I worked at Capital One as an HR person as well.

Basically, one day, I was at Capital One, working as an HR person. I did background screening for contractors. I dealt with a lot of third party vendors and things like that. We were putting together a deal, and I knew nothing about staffing, didn't know anything about the margins or anything like that. But I always knew I wanted to be an entrepreneur. Probably five, seven years before that, I owned a franchise, and I bought a franchise.

So I started trying to get my feet wet as an entrepreneur, running a business. I learned a lot in that business, and I lost a lot of money in that business. But I learned a lot. Moving fast-forward, at Capital One, I did a lot of background screening, working with third party vendors. I was trying to hire someone, and one of the reps said, "Hey, we can only pay this guy this much." I was like, "Well, you're paying him $21-22 an hour, but your invoice goes to $45 or $50. I started thinking, I was like, "Where's that other money going?" She's like, "Oh, that's our profit." So, I'm like, "You guys are making money off this guy." And you're just this company. I was like, they're just sitting there. So right then and there, bells went off. And I called my wife, and I was like, "You know what? I think I'm going to give this staffing thing a try, because it just made sense."

And so, I went home. I started learning about the industry a little bit, started the company. Still didn't really do anything with it, because I was still working at Capital One. Two years later, got laid off. Then, it was either find another corporate position or just go full of force there with my company. And, that's what I did. I just said, "Hey, I'm putting all my eggs in one basket, Gateway Integrated Solutions. And it's either going to work or it's not going to work." I knew I had a background in legal and HR, so I can get a job. I was like, I'm not going back to corporate America, so this has to work. It has to. And so, I took a lot of time to learn it. I did a lot of networking, took my bumps and bruises trying to get contracts on the public and private side. A lot of nos, I mean a bunch of nos. But that didn't deter me, because being prior military, I knew I had the discipline. I knew how to build a structure. I knew how to build a team.

And so, it just took me that time to build up to where I was able to win this one contract. And, it wasn't overnight. I'm on the calls with you guys all the time, and I know sometimes I may bug you on LinkedIn. I'd be like, "Hey, I want to do this, want to do that." The good thing about you is that you respond so quickly, and I know that you're busy. I was like, "Man, she's not going to answer me back right away." And, then I get my little message indicator. I said, "Oh, she emailed me back." So, I want to thank you for that. One of the things you always said was, "If you don't do it, if you don't bid, you don't know if you're going to win or if you're going to lose."

When I saw the proposal that I went after, I was in that position. I was like, "I have nothing to lose. I can either win it, and if I lose it, they'll debrief me. So then the next one I'll know what not to do." But, I was very strategic about this RFP because there was a lot of positions, with information, with IT people, and different types of skill sets.

So, I knew I was going up there against big companies. What I did was, I saw four roles that I knew I could dance. There were administrative support roles, but I was like, "Hey, with the margins there, because with the proposals, there was a 'not to exceed' limit." With the 'not to exceed' limit, that made me feel better, because I knew administrative individuals are getting anywhere from $18-20, $21 an hour. If their 'not to exceed limit' was $45-50, I was like, well these are some pretty decent margins.

I could feel one administrative support position, with that one role, then there may be 10 to 15 contractors per role. So, I could wind up actually getting anywhere from 40 to 50 people just on these four roles.

Dr. Kizzy Parks:

Right. Because I love this. Who was this contract for? Because I want to just quickly recap, serving in the military, and thank you for your service. You worked in all of these positions. You took two years to say, "Okay, I'm finally going to go out there." Then sometimes a door closes, and that's what happened. Layoff, "Hey, I'm going to make this work."

Steve Dixie:

Right.

Dr. Kizzy Parks:

Then you start, you're doing it, and then you get into the government contracting side. So, breakdown for all of us, who is this agency? What kind of roles? Tell us more, because this is exciting.

Steve Dixie:

Okay. Yeah, so it was with the State of South Dakota. And so it was an 'invite only'. How I got on that list, I have no idea. I have no clue. Only thing I know I do is respond to everything. Nothing comes across my email, I read everything and I respond to it. I read it, I respond.

And, that's one of the things that I've learned to do, is that if you respond, eventually someone is going to email you back, or say, "Hey, we're interested in your services." So that was the contract with the State of South Dakota. It was an 'invite only'. It wasn't any set aside, but I figured 'invite only' is just good as a set aside.

Dr. Kizzy Parks:

Right. That's key. I want to really emphasize that. That's super key, because like you said, even if you don't win, first off, you can't win if you don't take a chance. Even at the state level, they'll give debriefs, they'll give you some type of information. Okay, what were these positions for?

Steve Dixie:

So, the position was for administrative, it was administrative support, executive administration, and scanning. And, I think there was one for, I think, a data analyst. So, they were very simple positions, but the margins were there. And one thing I know is, I know there's one thing that I'm good at, and that's writing. And so, I knew how to write. I didn't know how to write a proposal, but being a paralegal, I knew when they ask a simple question, you give a simple answer.

Dr. Kizzy Parks:

Yep.

Steve Dixie:

And, a lot of people, they'll look at it, and they may ask you, "How many years have you done this?" And they'll go, "Well, I've done this, and this, and I've done that." And I just said, "I've done this for three years." Period. And that's it. I was very specific about what they wanted, what they asked.

One of the things you always said, if you don't have any experience, it's really not a problem. I haven't really staffed anywhere; I haven't staffed anyone. But, I have worked with different individuals in different companies, like with worldwide technology. And, I had some other guys that I worked with, and I helped with the pre-proposal. Even though they didn't win the award, I reached back out to those guys, "Hey, you asked me to do something. I fulfilled my agreement with you. Can you write me a past performance?" And they were like, "Sure." That's how I built up my past performance. It wasn't about how much money I had made on those guys, it was my performance while I was helping them do the pre-proposal. So, that came in handy, that's where my past performance came in.

Dr. Kizzy Parks:

I love that, because that is all about you demonstrating to South Dakota or whomever that you're able to do the thing: that's what they're looking for. The past performance isn't about how much money you made, did you get an award? Are you on the cover of a magazine? No, it's can you do it. Because the worst thing, we've all experienced it: you hire somebody to come in, it could be plumbing, it could be painting, it could be carpeting, and they leave, then you're like, "Man, I can't believe they did this. I could have done this better," or, you're like, "I thought that they had experience," or, "I thought the reviews were correct."

That's what they're trying to do, minimize risk. So, I love that you reached out in that way because the same applies to anyone who's ever subbed and subbed: you can still ask for past performance. You don't have to be the prime or the name on the marquee. Oh, I love this. Okay, keep going.

Steve Dixie:

So, I wrote the proposal, and they asked what type of software you use and different types of things, recruiting tools, recruiting software, so I had that in place, I had the structure in place, I had my payroll set up, I had my recruiting tools set up, so I was like, "This is who I'm using, this is what I've done in the past." Basically, that was it. And I took the time, I had to submit it on a totally different software that the State of South Dakota used. So I reached out, told them, I was like, "Hey, my proposal is ready, and can you give me the link or give me the information to submit it?"

They provided me with that and I just submitted it. And one of the things I did, I did contact the contracting officer, but I didn't bug her. I just said, "Hey, I'm interested in submitting a bid for this proposal. These are the roles that I want to submit it for," and I put four roles down here, and that was it.

Dr. Kizzy Parks:

How many did they have?

Steve Dixie:

Oh, it was probably about 70, 75.

Dr. Kizzy Parks:

Did they inform you that you could select for only a handful of labor categories?

Steve Dixie:

Yes.

Dr. Kizzy Parks:

I love that, because to your earlier point, even if you just fill one position, that could be tons of people.

Steve Dixie:

Right.

Dr. Kizzy Parks:

Even if it's a tiny state, even if it's New Hampshire, you don't know the volume of their needs.

Steve Dixie:

No, and the thing about this particular contract is that it's with a certain department. So, within that department, they have I think 12 to 15 offices throughout South Dakota. It's with the Department of Social Services of South Dakota. They have so many offices throughout South Dakota, and so I'm going through my mind, I was like, "Okay, if they can give me one person in each one of these locations for each one of these roads, I'm going to make some decent money."

Dr. Kizzy Parks:

You can make really good money.

Steve Dixie:

My brother, he's my go-to guy, he's an accountant, and so I just put the minimum down, I was like, "Hey man, can you just kind check the figures for me and let me know what you think I want to make on this?" So, we looked at it and it was in the seven figures, easy, just off a three-year contract, on a minimum.

Dr. Kizzy Parks:

Minimum. And that's the other thing: this isn't like reselling pens. You don't need to sell a million of these.

Steve Dixie:

No.

Dr. Kizzy Parks:

You can have one contract and you work that one contract, you're good. Because then, who knows? Maybe a year from now they're like, "Listen, we have this other opportunity with the universities, and we thought of you. It's 'invite only.'" Maybe they open up some new center, "Hey, we thought of you." It's not about the volume game: it's getting in with multi-year profitable work that you can really grow. Oh, my gosh.

Steve Dixie:

That was my plan, though. Like I said, I wrote it, I was very specific with it, I didn't hear anything back for a couple of months, but I think they said they was going to have the award date, I think the award date was 1 June, and so June that came by, and I was like, "Ah, I probably didn't get it," so I just started looking for something else to do, and then I think two or three weeks later I get an email saying, "Hey, we want to accept your bid. Here's the information that we're going to need from you. You should be receiving your contract within the next couple of weeks," so I've been working with them now. I've set up my direct deposit, I got a vendor number with them, so I'm just waiting on my contract to give me more details as to exactly how I'm going to fulfill it. So yeah, I'm excited about it. It's my first one. It took me forever.

But like you said, you have to stick with it. I don't have any backup. This is it for me, and I was telling my wife, we were talking one day and I was remembering this quote that Kobe said, they asked him, "You put all your eggs in one basket," and he was like, "Yeah." They were like, "Well, what happens? You get so many eggs," and he's like, "I get a bigger basket," and so that was my thing. I was like, "This is it for me. I don't have anything else. I got to make this work."

I was blessed to win those four little roles, but I feel comfortable with it. And being a prior contractor, I understand what they want and what they're needing as far as the pay and things like that. And, if you pay a contractor a good salary and not try to make so much money yourself, because you're going to make some money and staffing, that's just the bottom line, but if you're going to be greedy and not pay your contractors, you're going to have a high turnover. That's going to keep you busy recruiting.

And so, I think we have a pretty good hourly rate for each one of our positions. I don't think they're going to be running, and so we're excited about it. And again, I just wanted to thank you because once I got on with your team at GovCon Winners, things started to click a little bit more because you're learning in this business every day.

Dr. Kizzy Parks:

Yes. And I appreciate that. All the heavy lifting, all of it's you, and it's nice to have that mentor there because it clicks and it is learning. It's not, "Oh, I've been in GovCon for several years," or what may have you, "I know it all. Let me keep it moving," like, no: there's always something to learn at the state, local, federal, there's always something to learn.

I want to commend you because there are those out there that would've been like, "Oh, 70 labor positions. Where am I going to find these people?" and some people may not even know where South Dakota is on the map. Hey, I get it: it's not like the state we all are thinking about all the time, but at the end of the day, you're like, "Hey, but I can at least fill these four," and that probably meant the world to them because there's always those, it's like the Jack of all trades, Jane of all trades like, "Oh, I can do it all. I can fix your carpet, and your walls, and your plumbing, and I can build the garage you're looking for, and I can do your gardening," and you're like, "What?"

And so, it probably said a lot to them because they're like, "Oh wow, this is great. He pointed out these four," because we all appreciate somebody who can do something so well. They're not looking for just, "Meh." And especially, say, a state like South Dakota where you have parts that are very rural, and I imagine given the agency you're supporting, you're going to have positions maybe at or on reservations, you're going to have different locations in very rural areas. And so, they also realize that they don't want people to be taken advantage of and then they're going to be on the news, all that kind of stuff. So, I love the strategy that you applied because, look, you ended up winning.

Steve Dixie:

Yeah. And, one of the things that I thought about too was, one of the things that you mentioned was boots on the ground. In my process of trying to put together this proposal, I started picking out the roles I wanted and I was like, "Okay, would it be easier for me to staff an administrative person that's there, who can go on site, and be happy with the salary I give her? Or would it be easier for me to find a senior network engineer who's saying, "I'm not going to South Dakota. It has to be remote."

To me, it just made sense to help. You're probably doing something for the economy as well, because you're going to put some people to work there in South Dakota, and there's a few military bases there, and I know that a lot of dependent wives that they're looking for jobs like this because they're only there for three or four years, then they're moving on. So, the administrative part really hit me right, then I was like, "It's a lot easier to fill an administrative position in this region versus a senior network engineer," but yeah, if I go to DC it's different.

Dr. Kizzy Parks:

We're all different.

Steve Dixie:

But, in South Dakota, North Dakota, Iowa, and places like that, it's probably going to be simpler to fill administrative support positions. You have to humble yourself and be like, "Look, I know I can do this. This is what I can do. I know I'm a staffing agency. I know how to do this." This is what I could do. I know I'm a staffing agency. I know how to do this. I know how to recruit these people. Let me go do it. It ain't all about the high dollar margins or things like that because like you're saying, most importantly, you got to perform.

Dr. Kizzy Parks:

They'll take note of who is performing, who's providing the personnel, who is performing and showing up and doing everything that they want. One thing that comes up a lot is, oh, my background is legal or my background's psychology. I just stay in those areas or provide services in those areas. It's not so much your area as an expert, it's about that entrepreneurial hat.

Steve Dixie:

Right?

Dr. Kizzy Parks:

Identifying it makes it much easier to fill these types of positions, admins, etc., as opposed to IT, because then later you can win a contract to fill IT positions. Not only is it challenging in general, the other thing that often happens is getting different visas and having them sponsored. And, there are companies that are cool with that, but for something like this, it probably won't happen. And so then, somebody would have a contract for labor positions that they can't fill. It's almost like having a credit card that doesn't work, right? Or that person who has all the Bitcoin, but they don't know their key to their Bitcoin wallet. And, it's frustrating and it's aggravating. So, there are those times you have to humble yourself and say, "Okay, these are the positions." Because again, the money will come.

Steve Dixie:

Right. Exactly. Exactly.

Dr. Kizzy Parks:

What are some other things, because you talked about direct deposit, you talked about some paperwork? What are some other things that you've been going through to get set up with them?

Steve Dixie:

I did, of course, and you have to do your W-9. Everyone asks for a W-9. Once I got the W-9 set up, they set up my direct deposit. Then, they gave me a vendor number, because I didn't have a vendor number within the state. So, they set that up. That's it that I've so far and I've been in contact. Well, the contracting officer emailed me saying, "Hey, you should be receiving your contract." But, then when I should be receiving it, I thought I would have it today, but she said, "You'll have it this week," which I was like, that's fine. I know it's coming. I know it's there, so I'm not too worried about it now. She was like, "We're going to get it to you." So, that's what I'm waiting on right now, just to contract itself. I have that going and I just try to keep myself busy with other things as well.

Dr. Kizzy Parks:

This is really common, too. There are times where you wait, they have to get everything together. There are times where in your email there's a contract, but very similar to the federal side is they pay through direct deposit. That's why it's key to have your business banking set up, have all of that stuff already done, because you don't have to have a bank in that state. And then, something that you could do if you wanted to, but you don't have to, is register in South Dakota as a business. They may require it, they may not. Every place is different. That's the other thing, because you don't live in South Dakota.

Steve Dixie:

That was it. That was one of the things I was worried about.

Dr. Kizzy Parks:

But, at the same time, it helps them because maybe they're like, "We want to do something different." And so, that's the other big takeaway from this: you don't have to live there. No different than a federal contract. You don't have to live in that city, live in that state. Think of all of the businesses we patronize. How many of us purchase from Amazon and there's no Amazon warehouse in your city. They don't have to be there. That's the beauty of it. Now, if they require in the solicitation some things about city location, all of that, that's something you're going to have to work out, decide if you want to bid. So I further commend you because we get caught up in these sexy states, whatever may be sexy to you. I think New York or California or Florida. And it's like, don't overlook the Dakotas, Washington state is another big state that has a ton of work. Oregon. I didn't even ask this: how did you find out about this opportunity? We got the invite. Where would you normally go to find these different state-level opportunities?

Steve Dixie:

I go to SAM.gov a lot too, but then I also go to state. I'm in Nashville, Tennessee, so I look at Kentucky, I look at different government sites. I look at all government sites and I register for different networking or seminars. And they're online, they're virtual. And that's another thing, if you can go to any virtual seminars, I don't care where it is, I would go, because what happens is that while they're talking about, "Hey, this is what upcoming contracts we may have in the state of South Dakota." We're in the chat putting out business information in that with different companies. And so, the people that are there, they're saying, "Hey, okay, here's Steve. He's in Nashville and he has a staffing company." So, you register with each one of these states.

And that's how I do. I go to each state when I see somebody saying, "Hey." I get a lot of stuff from VA and everybody says, "Hey, we're having a virtual event out of Nevada. Would you be interested?" I'm signing up for it. I don't care because you just never know. And that's what I do. Whenever the VA sends me something or any other type of entity sends me something about a virtual seminar, I definitely sign up and I attend it because that's how you get on their radar.

Dr. Kizzy Parks:

It is! It also shows you the sheer amount of competition. We think, "Oh, why would they ever pick me? Why would a state or agency, why would they pick me?" Why wouldn't they pick you? That's how it should be. Why shouldn't they pick you? And so then you may think, "Well, but there's so much competition." And then you go to these events and what did you notice? Were there thousands of people in attendance?

Steve Dixie:

No, no, it's not. There may be like 15 or 20 companies there. It's a virtual event. And this is this thing, that once you register on those sites, you start getting emails from those different states. They'll be like, "Hey, we're having another event for a certain type of staffing or thing that we're looking for services or product that we're looking for." And sometimes, it's like things that I can't do, but I still receive the emails. And if I know people that I know that can do that type of work, I would send it to them because I'm not a consultant. And so, that's something that I don't do. And one guy asked me, I was doing something, he was like, "Hey, can you do consultant work?" I was like,"No, that's not in my lane." And I'm not stepping out. I'm not going to try to learn that while I'm trying to learn this. I could be making this over here in my wheelhouse, so I stay focused on what I'm supposed to do. That's how I got the most. Like I said, I go to different state agencies, I just see what they have. You can navigate through those state agencies a lot easier than you can through SAM.gov because you could spend two, three days looking through SAM.gov and never find anything. But you can go to these state agencies and find something like that.

Dr. Kizzy Parks:

You sure can. And that's why I like the balance. Even my flagship company, we're getting more into state-level because we're on a subcontract with the state we staff. For instance, we have a tutor in Spanish for the surgeon general of Florida.

Steve Dixie:

Of course.

Dr. Kizzy Parks:

We have all these different positions. But, I've noticed that too. I've been going out there. And the thing is, especially those of you where you're like, "Oh, I don't want to put out a lot of money." Registering with these states costs nothing.

Steve Dixie:

Nothing, nothing.

Dr. Kizzy Parks:

It costs nothing. And then when you're really laser focused and all you're looking at is Tennessee or Oklahoma or Kentucky, you're laser focused and they're going to post them there probably much faster. And even if you use some other paid site, plus, there may be other information they're going to notify you or they may share about the events that you were talking about. And that's amazing, because they're going to want to do business with the people they keep seeing at the events. It shows them, "Oh wow, they really know about us and we're Idaho. I can't believe that Steve keeps coming to these." This is pretty interesting because they know there are people in their states, and when I say people, I mean individuals, companies who they're not looking to do work there, and so they have a need and they're looking for each and every one of us to fulfill that. I love this. What are some types of efforts that you're chasing right now?

Steve Dixie:

I started working on a GSA schedule. I have already submitted my offer for a GSA schedule, so I'm just waiting to hear back from that. Hopefully this week. I just talked to the contracting officer on Friday. That was another one where just being blessed, a friend of mine that I knew that was in Virginia, she got me in on it. It was a pilot program, it was an east pilot program through the GSA. So where it normally takes three to six months to get a GSA contract, this program, you get a contract within eight to 12 weeks, but you have to do the work. I mean, you have to do it. And the good thing about that was you get assigned one representative up at the GSA level. It was three intakes. Intake form one, intake form two and three. So with each intake form you have to kind of answer questions again. You have to answer questions and I would email it, take my time, write it. She was like you may want to add this, you may want to do this.

So, once you get through that step process, then you get to the next process. This is where you have to be really confident in yourself and find ways to move around the system. I had no income with Gateway, none. And so, that was one of the requirements. She was like, you don't have any income. I was like, no, but I was introduced to a guy who owns a funding company and I was like, look, this is what I'm trying to do. I'm trying to get on a GSA schedule. I explained it to them, I was like, can you give me a line of credit? Don't base it off my personal credit. Can you base it off of the contract that I'm going to get? And so, I got a pretty significant amount of line of credit. I submitted that letter from the funding company versus invoices and so she was like, okay, this will work.

So, that was my only concern. And then once I got past that, I completed all the three phases and so she was like, okay, you can go ahead and submit your offer now. And so, there's three positions that I put. I picked a talent acquisition manager, HR manager, and associate recruiter. And so within those three roles, I can go to any company and be like, hey, we have the structure set up. We've been vetted through the GSA, here's our schedule. If it's a government agency, we can staff 20 people because we have the structure already in play. I'm your HR person, basically. You're the guru of that.

Dr. Kizzy Parks:

This is good for everyone, because, once again, it's not about your GSA schedule encompassing every single thing the government buys. It's also great that you took advantage of a pilot program that costs you that amount of money, zero. And what's key is with the GSA schedule, once you get in there, you can modify it.

Steve Dixie:

Yes.

Dr. Kizzy Parks:

Let's say three years from now, you may want to add 150 different labor categories.

Steve Dixie:

Right.

Dr. Kizzy Parks:

We want to apply for other schedules. That's what's golden. And it's great because you can leverage that for people to team with you. For instance, we're going through something right now where the reason the company's teaming with us, they're not small, and it's on the GSA schedule, so they need somebody like us to partner with. It happens all of the time. So, I love that you're doing that. Love that. And, I love that you use the line of credit because again, it shows it's not about, oh, I've billed billions of dollars and here are my invoices, or I have 20,000 years experience staffing a million people. It's about what can you demonstrate that minimizes risk? You did it because you got that line of credit, and because the GSA schedule is all about that he's been vetted, he's going to deliver. There's nothing for you to worry about. So, the line of credit, in my opinion, is even stronger than invoices because who knows what's going on behind the scenes with the invoices?

Steve Dixie:

Exactly. I learned a lot about the ledger line of credit versus just the regular line of credit. So like I said, you learn something every day in this business, and that was something that really helped me out. One of the other companies that I helped do a pre-proposal for, they reached out to me and were like, hey, would you like to do a joint venture? And so I was like, sure, because I have certifications, which of course they don't have. And I was like, oh, they did all the paperwork. They set up the joint venture company. It took three years and everything started to come to fruition all at the same time it seemed. And that's why I said, you can't give up. You just have to keep moving.

Don't get me wrong now, there were times that I was like, man, I don't know if this is going to work. You have those days. Then I was like, what else can I do? And so, I would get back on it again though, I was blessed. Everything came to fruition at that one time. I have those three things going. That's it. I'm not doing anything else for right now. I'm not looking for any more work. Right now, I'm just trying to perform and that's it.

Dr. Kizzy Parks:

I'm so proud of you. That's all you've got to do is perform. The money will come and it will grow.

She Made $5 Million In Government Contracts In 12 Months - Leilani Lacusong

Kizzy:

We are in for a treat today. We have Ms. Leilani Lacusong, who is here to talk about how she went from a few hundreds of thousands of dollars a year to well over $3M in one year alone in federal government contracts, as well as how you can do that, too. I'm going to go ahead and turn this over to her, so she can formally introduce herself and tell us more all about her company, Leis Consulting.

Leilani:

It's an honor to be here with my mentor, officially.

Kizzy:

Aw, you're so sweet!

Leilani:

Well, it's definitely a journey, starting with revenue of $100 to $300 to $500K to $3M. I say...well, to five million 'cause the year's not over yet, you know?

Kizzy:

Right. That's right. The year's not over yet.

Leilani:

I'm not a fiscal year (company), we are a calendar year company. So, we are going to reach $5M to perhaps $5B! Okay, that's gonna be a secret.

Kizzy:

Tell us about what you do at Leis Consulting.

Leilani:

We are a general construction company, and I would say it took me about, I would say, four years to be in construction. It's definitely, I would say, a male dominant industry and especially... I'm in California. It was very challenging to get into the space because, definitely, I'm a woman and there's no space for me in construction. However, because of my diligence and...it was a capability briefing... and the CEO pulled me to the side and said, "Leilani, your passion is coming out of your pores."

So, I said, "You know what, can I steal that during my capability briefing?" He said, "Absolutely."

Kizzy:

(laughs)

Leilani:

So, from that point on, I was able to use that as an excuse to get in. Not an excuse, but I was able to get into the federal sector, and they really saw my sincerity, my authenticity, and my transparency when it comes to budgeting.

Kizzy:

Which is really key, because often we think that you lead with just the technical background, as opposed to these other elements, the passion or personality. So, some may think, like, "Oh, well, maybe she was already in construction." Were you in construction? How did you get into construction and this whole government contracting realm?

Leilani:

So, at the age of 17, I've worked for, I would say, four international firms, not to mention, you know, as a project accountant and also a project manager. I extracted all that skillset and I said, "You know what, I wear many hats!" And so, I extracted all the experiences that I have had, and I just, you know, I put them all in. I would say I put them in one jar and then I gave it to the federal government pretty much, not only the accounting side, but also the project management side and operating the company as a director of operations, and put all that in one bottle and sold it to the government.

Kizzy:

And what led to you going from being in these corporate environments to stepping out and being a business owner and providing construction to the federal government?

Leilani:

Because discrimination and they said I can't do it.

Kizzy:

Who said that?

Leilani:

I can't do it, meaning everybody. Coming from a W2 environment and the other general contractors, and they said, "You can't do it. You don't wanna do construction, you wanna do janitorial. You wanna advocate for the homeless." They said, "Leilani, there's just no way you can do it." And I said, "Okay." I said, "I'll be right back...," just to let them know that the more they challenge me by saying that I can't do it, they tell me to go right, and I go left.

Kizzy:

Which is a testament to you, because especially when you started out, you're dealing with being in an environment where most of the people don't look like you, where people are saying, "Hey, you're not gonna be able to do this. Why are you even trying?" Then, in this environment where you're making hundreds of thousands, you're making money, which seems like a lot for some. Hundreds of thousands of dollars is your ultimate goal. But keeping in mind, when the government spends well over 500 billion, hundreds of thousands is at the low end. So, what kept you going to keep you on this path to where you are now? Why not just say, "You know what, this is it?"

Leilani:

It's also a paradigm shift for me. It's not just knowing how you read the contracts or knowing the scope of work. But, I think it's a paradigm shift because I'm the product. I believed in myself because of the passion that I have. The people heard me on the phone, they see me while I'm on the phone, 'cause they never see me. Passion transcends the other party, and they said, "We gotta give her a chance."

I'm okay with a five-dollar contract, 10 dollars contract. But, I said, "Hey, this is a government contract." And, going back to my first original contract, it was $65,000 for five years.

Kizzy:

Wow!

Leilani:

So, let's call it a credit card drop.

Kizzy:

So, break that down. What was the contract for? Was there a particular set aside? How did they pay you?

Leilani:

Okay. It was definitely a set aside for a total small business. And I said, "You know what, take away all my experiences and other certifications, but I know how to compete. Let me compete." And, I've always been competitive even in the high school days and college days, and I just know I have it.

I just didn't know when I'm going to arrive. I just know I have this. I have this product that I can sell and somebody's gonna buy it. So, having said that, um, I just didn't stop.

Kizzy:

What is the agency?

Leilani:

It's the Air Force base in Dyess, Texas, and I didn't even know that Dyess, Texas, existed until I got there. It's for carpet extraction. Like, Lord, they need to do something-

Kizzy:

(laughs)

Leilani:

... with this (laughs). But, you know, I was happy cleaning the carpets because...none of my employees showed up on my first day.

Kizzy:

Wait, what? So, you get this five year contract for $65,000, you're ecstatic, you won, small business set aside, you're there in rural Texas, right?

Leilani:

Yes, ma'am.

Kizzy:

And no one shows up.

Leilani:

On my first day. I was at the welcome center. It was me and my carpet cleaning machine.

Kizzy:

Whoa!

Leilani:

It has built-in heat, by the way. Yes. So, who did you think extracted the dirt from the carpet? Me.

Kizzy:

I know. Yes, you.

Leilani:

Yes. Yes, ma'am. I was happy to do it. I was happy to do it. I was passionate, extracting that carpet for the next contract.

Kizzy:

In five years.

Leilani:

I said, "They're gonna see me. They're gonna know that I'm really passionate and this is my space. This is where I belong,

100% federal work." I have nothing against the state and the county, and I love my state and my city. But, I love being in this space. And that's how passionate I am.

Kizzy:

And it comes through, I mean, to the government employee who mentioned he could feel your passion to just being here with you, 'cause we're physically together here in California where you're crushing it. It's also vital, because it helps you stand out. There are thousands and thousands of different vendors out there, but how many people are actually passionate about what they do? I can even feel your passion talking about cleaning carpets where others may just see it and it's just, "Oh, you're cleaning carpets." It's like, "No, it's bigger than that." That's why you're beyond the million dollar mark. You know, fewer than 3% of women-owned businesses ever, ever, ever go past a million dollars in revenue. It's a huge accomplishment.

Leilani:

And, the difference is I was willing to do everything and anything beyond the scope. I was picking up trash and I know they can see me. They can see me like, "That's not part of my scope." I will clean the place like I have done and perform janitorial work. However, I said, "You know what? It's not part of my scope, don't do it." I was happy to do it. I was happy to break my back for the federal government.

Kizzy:

Wow.

Leilani:

Whenever it may be.

Kizzy:

And now you're in the 8(a) program.

Leilani:

Yes, I am.

Kizzy:

So, talk to us about that. So you won the first small business set-aside, and then how did you go from that to, "Okay, I'm going to get into this 8(a) program?"

Leilani:

Well, I had a story, not to mention sad moments during the 8(a), but I'm going to fast-forward it to the 8(a). I don't even know where to start, but I lost hope with the 8(a) program. It didn't matter to me what an 8(a) program is. I just didn't believe in the 8(a) program in the beginning.

Even now, because I would always advertise Leis Consulting Group, and we are dedicated and passionate about doing government contracting. Not just government contracting, because we are passionate about doing construction work.

Then, I realized that one of the agencies really, really saw me out, like, really saw what I was doing in their space. And, they said, "Leilani, you have to tell them that you are an 8(a). Don't dismiss that opportunity" and like, "Grow your business. Stop collaborating with the big guys, grow your business." And I thought, "Hey, when we collaborate, it will give you a better buffer, a better chance of winning." But no, if you're ready to, I would always say this, from California to Alaska, you can grow your business. And, that's how I grew my business.

Kizzy:

That is powerful, because the big businesses come across as shiny and stable, and we're often pushed or 'voluntold,' you know, "Go partner with one of these types of companies." But, there are these multi-billion dollar organizations where, in reality, what is our real value to them? Sometimes, they're working to take our work away or they just want to work with us because of our set-asides, and while it can be beneficial, it can also be very problematic.

Leilani:

Yes, and I have to thank you because it's not like you didn't coach me.

Kizzy:

(laughs).

Leilani:

You're like, "You know what, Leilani, go ahead, do your thing." You trusted me in that space. But also, sometimes you would warn me, "Uh, Leilani, don't do it." But, I was very stubborn. And so, it's one of those lessons learned, you know, and I wanted to have a taste of, not so much failure, but I wanted to have a taste so I could tell the other small businesses that, do not be so desperate to partner with a very huge firm, just try to grow your business. Start from humble beginnings and work your way up. There's nothing wrong with that.

Kizzy:

And that's what you've done, you know, as we worked together, and as I've been coaching amazing Leilani, is that she's focused on her business and on her team because, again, we get distracted. "Oh, this big company has this opportunity for us, so let's go over there." Or, "Oh, I wanna help out my cousin, so what can I do to win some work for my cousin?" Or, "Oh, I wanna focus on bidding, getting an 8(a) or a service disabled." And, we forget the main thing with business is sales. It's on building your business, because at the end of the day, it's your business.

So, what were some things about your capability brief journey? I don't know if I'm reading into it, but I feel like it's one of the pivotal points with you and your business as you were growing your business.

Leilani:

Okay. So, wow, I was really scared. I thought I was gonna pass out, because I said, "Okay, we're going to Texas and I'm gonna do a capability, not so much a capability briefing, but a 'capability gratitude' briefing, because people are telling me, "Leilani, the agency is familiar with you." But, I'm like, "Well, I haven't seen them. I wanna connect with them." So, by the time I got there, I just wanted to thank them for trusting me on a government contract. I'm like, "Wow, I feel so special." You know, because, I mean, it's the government. The federal government really wanted to trust me, my firm, to be able to do the work. We were also after a project which is really pivoting into another, I would say, not sector, but another venture with Kizzy,, which is staffing.

And I really... Like, in my mind, we already won the contract, when we came back from Texas to California, I said, "We have to be in the Qualified Vendors List (QVL), otherwise, how am I going to redeem myself?" I was nervous that I have to talk to the FAA behind the scenes because if I don't get into the QVL, I'm, like, "Holy, holy, shit."

Kizzy:

(laughs).

Leilani:

(laughs) I'm sorry.

Kizzy:

That's all right.

Leilani:

But we did it, you know. I already knew that we were gonna get in, because Dr. Parks has years and years of experience in this space. But one thing is, I know we were talking about government contracting. We were talking about how to be successful, how to be a great entrepreneur, but I think I also did put my mindset into really, it's when they say, "You walk the walk," you know?

I would say, I breathe, I ate to SAM.gov. And that's the honest to God truth. I wore my shirt every day, I'm Leis consulting 24/7. I'm not Leilani, but I was Leis Consulting Group. And, I did it seven days a week. Non-stop. For seven years, non-stop.

Kizzy:

Wow!

Leilani:

And, I would always say, "It's a lonely place to be."

Kizzy:

But you never gave up?

Leilani:

No.

Kizzy:

And that's what's so important about this, is that she never gave up, she's been crushing it with the Federal Aviation Administration (FAA). I knew that it was just a matter of just adding a technique, strategies, and the 'why behind why' these strategies actually work.

So, when we were in Texas with the FAA, what was amazing

about the small business rep was that there were, I believe, three contracting officers. It was great, because they were able to meet Leilani. I played a minor role, and I told her she (Leilani) was Beyonce, I was just Kelly Rowlands over here. Leilani was the main person, and I was just there just serving as her mentor, just being there for support.

What's also key is, in addition to where you're going, it's important to look into different areas to branch off into, and so staffing was one of them. You can share with the world, "Oh, I wanna do staffing," or, "I wanna sell products." But, you know, are they really going to believe you? But, when you go there with someone who has a track record of it, it really shows them, "Oh, wow. Okay, now we can think of Leis Consulting Group as a thing, as providing staffing and construction. Not just because she said it, we see it." Then, that teed us up to partner on an opportunity that's at least a $1 billion for this QVL that we're on?

Leilani:

$5 billion, or five years, yes. But, it's just not the contracts, you know, when you're starting your business. Not just the contracts, not just the relationships. I look at it like in construction, what is your foundation? Who are you with? Who's around you? Who's your network? Who's your family? Loyalty, for me, is very important, so...this part, I promise not to cry, I really promise not to cry and shed any tears.

But, I must say, if you're starting your business, and this is the honest to God truth, I was in debt building my company, $250K, and I said, "Shoot. I can't have a finance accounting background and I'm in debt." So, what is important is you have to find a family, 'cause family for me is very important. I don't have a big family, but I'm married to SAM.gov.

Kizzy:

(laughs).

Leilani:

That's my husband, by the way. SAM.gov is my husband. It is very important to have a village. A village will not let you fail. A village will not stab you in the back. A village will support you in any kind of way, however it can support you, it will be there. So, to me, that was important.

When Dr. Parks came...well, when I reached out to her, she actually gave me a brand new brain. And I'm not kidding, a brand new brain, my organs were chopped up, and she put me back together. Now, you get the brand new Leilani. I'm not saying that 'cause you're also my friend. Because I remembered those days during my broke, broke... during the time that I was breaking, you know, really I was not breaking down, but, yeah, I was sad. Thought I was going through depression there, I've never been depressed. But Kizzy, you know, I thank you. Because I remember a Saturday and a Sunday.... Okay, I'm not gonna cry, I promise. And you have a life, and the millions of subscribers that you have, and the people you mentor, but you stayed with me on the phone for Saturday and Sunday, and every weekend after that.

So, I'm forever, forever grateful for you.

Kizzy:

Well, I'm so appreciative!

Leilani:

So it's not so much, like, the whole mentorship, like I feel like I have a sisterhood with Kizzy. And, you know, it's like when you find your own family, you have your new ocean. And really, it makes your job out there lighter than what you think. Federal government contracting is not really that hard. But if you have the tenacity and the passion, there's no way that you cannot win your first federal contract.

Kizzy:

Winning is the easiest. But then, it's once you win, it's the executing, it's going from hundreds of thousands to millions, it's being to create this sisterhood. And, you ran with it. There are many out there who may have faced similar obstacles and they just gave up, and they said, "I'm done." And they didn't want to go forward. But you continued to persevere, and that's why you're at well over $3M, on track to $5M, because of that. Not just because of the 8(a) program, or maybe you're thinking, "Oh, she's just getting a ton of sole source work." That's not it at all. She also has a HUBZone, she also is competitively bidding, she's expanding. That's what makes a great company, to your point about the foundation, that's a strong foundation. These big companies, IBM, Lockheed Martin, Deloitte, they don't just provide one or two or three things, or one, and two, three verticals, they're in so many verticals.

Leilani:

That's true. And, like what she always say, "What is your added value?" So, once you build the foundation, you're like, "Wow, this is my added value." Then, you go to those big guys, and maybe they'll even entertain you. But with me, I'm just happy being in this space. I'm happy not even to reach out to the big guys out there. That's fine. I can be the little guy, it's not a problem. But this little guy got in the QVL.

Kizzy:

Right! Got into the QVL. And, you're working on projects that are so meaningful. Personally, I always had this kind of thought around construction, because I was not around anyone in construction when I first started out in government contracting. I had no idea. Everyone was in simulations in Orlando, they were in training, they were in staffing, they were in IT. And so, I also have learned a ton from you, because I learned the meaning.

You know, you want to talk about the tower project that you're working on?

Leilani:

Yeah...actually, our team is going to repair the air tower control in Yakima, Washington. It's an amazing job. I don't know how much more that I can share. We're going to Yakima tonight. And I will just say, just an amazing project. I feel privileged to be in this space, to be able to work with the federal government. You know? It's like going into, Disneyland or Disney World and you're like, "Oh my God, all these rides!"

Kizzy:

(laughs)

Leilani:

...you know, that's how I felt. You know? It's just really super amazing, the awareness that I have that other people don't have. It's like it's a forever weapon that I have that nobody can take it away from me.

Kizzy:

And they can't! They can't take it away. You're working on these efforts, they're so important, which is amazing. Because I think that's one of the greatest things about federal government contracting. It's not just, "Oh, I sold some computer parts on Amazon," which is amazing if that's what you do too. But, this is meaningful, and what she's going to work on there is going to have an impact on the community. That's just what's so awesome about this space and the options.

You know, I always talk about it's like a cereal aisle, because I used to always love eating lots of cereal. Like, Cocoa Puffs when I was a little girl.

Leilani:

Fruity Pebbles (laughs).

Kizzy:

So, you have so many options, and that's what's so cool. And, just especially going back to your background in finance, and then bam, you're in construction.

Leilani:

Yes. But I also, I would say, I grew up, since I was 17, being around architecture, architects, engineers, and construction. I just didn't know I was in that space. I'm like, how are they getting all these projects? It was in front of me, but I wasn't aware. Awareness is the key. Now, I'm aware that this is actually possible. It's possible to work with the government. It's just super amazing.

I wanted to say, with all sincerity to you, Kizzy, that this newfound ocean for me, I want to talk about how easy it is and how it's less challenging for me to be in this space knowing that you have support. Knowing that you can call someone, knowing that I can call you at any time, even though hundreds of people are probably calling you per day. But, you don't fail to respond to me. So, thank you.

Kizzy:

Aw!

Leilani:

Thank you, thank you. And to your team, you know. You have an amazing team, you have an amazing company. I wanted to tell everyone too, that, in researching for your mentor or someone, I would say, for your newfound family, right, it's very important that you look at their winnings, too. How can they teach you? Kizzy, I mean, you guys probably already know that you won over $50M in contracts. So I'm like, "How did she do that?" She actually did it, it's her company. So. I just wanted to say, I mean I sound like a broken record, but family's important.

Kizzy:

It is! I appreciate what you said, and it's what you put in the work. The biggest piece is that you don't give up, you put in the work, you keep the questions coming, because every single situation is different. Even within the same agency, even within the same body of work. So make sure you also give yourself flowers for all of your accomplishments and you're going to continue doing. I'm just so grateful because you make it easy.

Leilani:

Thank you.

Kizzy:

And I love that, and that's also why I'm pretty sure, especially after what I saw at the FAA with the capability briefing experience, you make it easy for them. That's why they were open to meeting with you. That's why they had the three contracting officers there and the small business rep. Because they want us to make it easy. They don't want us to stand in the way or to be on this pedestal. They want somebody like Leilani, like y'all watching. You know? So, I'm just so grateful. Thank you.

Where can people go if they want to get in contact with you, or maybe they want to subcontract or they just want to learn?

Leilani:

They can go to my website. They didn't have any available domains, so. The hyphen in between the Leis consulting group dot com. So it's Leis-Consulting-Group.com.

Kizzy:

I love it, again, that you make the most of what's there. Thank you!

CHAPTER 7

ROBUST RESOURCES

Venturing into the realm of government contracting can be both a lucrative and fun-filled endeavor. As new contractors attempt to carve niches for themselves in this specialized market, understanding and accessing a vast array of resources becomes crucial.

Stepping into this vast world of information, tools, and assets can often feel like navigating a maze. Recognizing this, I've curated a list of resources to meet your specific needs and interests. From a plethora of domains, these resources stand as testaments to my commitment to aiding your journey, whatever that might entail. I invite you to delve into this list, confident that you'll find elements that resonate with you regarding your objectives and ambitions. #EverythingisPossible!

GovCon Winners™ YouTube channel

www.youtube.com/@KizzyParks

GovCon Winners™ Facebook Group

www.facebook.com/groups/gcwalways

APEX Accelerators program

www.apexaccelerators.us/#

Apply for Set-Asides

certify.sba.gov

DIBBS (DLA Internet Bid Board System)

www.dibbs.bsm.dla.mil/dodwarning.aspx?goto=/rfq

Domains for Sale

www.godaddy.com

FedConnect

www.fedconnect.net/FedConnect/Default.htm

Federal Procurement Data System

www.fpds.gov/fpdsng_cms/index.php/en

Free EIN Registration

www.irs.gov/businesses/small-businesses-self-employed/how-to-apply-for-an-ein

Free Logo

www.brandcrowd.com

FREE SBA Program

sba7j.fedbidspeed.com

GPO (Government Publishing Office)

www.gpo.gov/how-to-work-with-us/vendors/programs-for-vendors

Grants.gov

www.grants.gov

GSA's AAAP (Automated Advanced Acquisition Platform)

leasing.gsa.gov/leasing/s

GSA's RSAP (Requirement Specific Acquisition Platform)

leasing.gsa.gov/leasing/s/RSAP-PortalHome

LinkedIn

www.linkedin.com

President Biden supports small business owners

www.sba.gov/article/2023/07/18/biden-harris-administration-sets-record-breaking-163-billion-federal-procurement-opportunities-small#:~:text=Releasing%20new%20guidance%2C%20%E2%80%9CCreating%20a,Dashboard%20to%20track%20an%20agency%27s

Pricing Help

buy.gsa.gov/pricing

Register as a seller with Unison

marketplace.unisonglobal.com/sellerregistration.flow?execution=e1s1

Register to Vote!

www.vote.org

SAM.gov

sam.gov/content/home

Small Business Administration (SBA) contracting assistance programs

www.sba.gov/federal-contracting/contracting-assistance-programs

Sign up with GovCon Winners

www.govconwinners.com

WHERE TO GO FROM HERE

Congratulations! If you've read this book, you are now armed with the basic knowledge of how to be successful in federal government contracting. In reading the preceding chapters, you've learned about the strategies I've developed over many years to become successful in federal government contracting and how I've helped hundreds of selected clients become successful in it, as well. So, you're all set, and you're going to make millions right away, right?

Not yet! While I've explained the basic rules and pathways to becoming successful in this business, it won't magically happen just because of your newfound knowledge. You can mix all these ingredients together that I've laid out on the table before you, but just like the chef in the kitchen preparing any meal, all the difference is in that chef-and that's you. YOU are the catalyst in landing those contracts that can change your life for the better. YOU are the change agent who can make it all happen-or not! YOU have to do the work, get out there, and take charge of your future, because reading a book will never be enough. YOU have to make the positive change in your life to get the kind of success that I know you want for yourself and your families.

So, get out there and do it! The entire point of this book has been to serve as a confidence builder for you to know that you can do this. Keep this book by your side and use it as a handy reference for when you need to refresh your recollection or re-motivate yourself. Success in life rarely comes before committing to and working toward a goal that will get you there.

There's nothing special about me or the many others who have been successful in this business. The difference has been having the dream, showing the tenacity to plan and work for that dream, and then following through. Think of yourself as an athlete, training to achieve a specific metric in performance. Think of your own educational and work achievements, and how you followed a plan and took the time and effort to achieve that diploma, certificate, or promotion. And now, think of yourself before you picked up this book and how you'll feel after you've finished reading it.

Because even though it's a cliche, it's a good one: every journey begins with a single step. You took that step when you cracked open this book and kept reading to this point. Now, it's time to follow the steps laid out in this book and establish your own financial success. I'm here to help, and so are many others, with the references I provided earlier. If you feel you need coaching or mentoring, I can help you there, too.

The best part, however, is that you did this by yourself. You picked up this book, you read it, and if you're still interested and motivated, there's a pathway before you to follow. The next step is up to you. You have the knowledge now, and with what you've accomplished so far in life, you know it's in you to do this.

Join my Facebook group. Watch my YouTube videos. Take advantage of the FREE resources I cited earlier. And, if you feel you would benefit from it, look into getting a coach or mentor, such as myself or someone else with the right knowledge you trust. And, you can text me at (305) 853-9481 anytime.

#EverythingisPossible!

ABOUT THE AUTHOR

As a kid, I cleaned the golf balls that were hit over the fence of the local golf course and into an alley behind my friend's house. I then sold those golf balls to golfers through the fence and used the money to buy snacks such as FUNYUNS® and Nutty Bars.

I always knew I'd become an entrepreneur as well as earn an advanced degree in psychology. My entrepreneurial spirit meshed well with my inquisitive nature as an adopted child, who always wanted to, and then met, her birth family. Driven to be the successful business owner I always knew I would be, I went on to earn a Ph.D. and establish KPC, my flagship company, over a decade ago.

I own and operate multiple businesses and have won over $75M in federal government contracts. My students have won over $3M in federal government contracts in under six months. With my proven methods and track record of success, I will help YOU, too, via the GovCon Winners ™ strategy!

FUN FACT:

I'm a GUINNESS WORLD RECORDS™ titleholder!

TEXT me at (305) 853-9481

Printed in the USA
CPSIA information can be obtained
at www.ICGtesting.com
CBHW061705100924
14059CB00073B/2486